AF333143

Letters Through The Veil

Letters Through The Veil

By Loryn "Solana" Walton

Solstar
P.O. Box 320987
Cocoa Beach, FL 32932-0987
Solstarpub@aol.com

Letters Through The Veil

PRINTING HISTORY
First Printing 2000

ISBN 0-9679779-0-8

PRINTED IN THE UNITED STATES OF AMERICA
1 2 3 4 5 6 7 8 9 10

Library of Congress Card Number: 00-102802

This book is dedicated to God....

And to all those that seek the truth....

*Love outlasts death
and the ravages of time.*
-Paramahansa Yogananda

Acknowledgments

I express my gratitude to all the teachers that have influenced my life especially: Swami Satchidananda, Paramahansa Yogananda, Babaji, Jose Silva, Claire Kenna, Patricia Hayes, Marshall Smith, Mauricio Panisset, Gary Bonnell, Robert Monroe, Wayne Dyer, Charles and Caroline Muir, and Frank Natale.

I would like to offer my appreciation to my sister Mari McTaggart who guided and supported me in numerous ways and her husband Richard McTaggart who graciously offered me a place in their home. Also, to my other family members who have helped and encouraged me, Brenda Martin, Stevan and Corinne Martin, David Martin, Martin B. Martin, Eva Costa, and Stephanie and Rocco Patel. A heartfelt thanks goes to Donna Weycker, Mike Cook, Surya and Leela Lipscombe, Bruce Rempel, Terry Woerner, Peggie Grace Coffey, and Ray Dickinson for their help and support; to Pat O'Neil, Jim Roaché, Frank Hudak, Crystal Holton, and Robin Nelson for their knowledge in the publishing and editing business, to Mickey Trione for his artistic abilities and to Linda Schurman and Debbie Ritchie for their intuitive guidance.

Table of Contents

<u>*Letter to the Reader*</u>

Dear Reader,

In Hawaii, on June 28, 1995, I married the man of my dreams. I thought we would live happily ever after in Paradise. For three weeks I lived in a state of bliss and gratitude. Then, at the age of thirty-three, my husband, Rock, unexpectedly died of a heart attack. I was totally traumatized and kept hoping I would wake up from the nightmare. I fell into a deep depression, having no idea if I would ever find my way out again.

In the middle of the night, after his death, I woke up hearing his voice in my head. He was singing the words of our wedding song to me. He continued to comfort me all through the night. I felt his presence whenever I was alone. It was difficult for me to talk about our communication with others because of their skepticism. I searched for books that might confirm my experiences and found none.

A year later, an inner voice urged me to write letters to my husband. I found it to be a profoundly healing experience. One day as I was writing about a challenging situation, I sensed Rock offering me guidance. For the first time I transcribed his letters *to* me thus beginning the Letters through the Veil, a record of our correspondence back and forth between the two worlds. At first, he only came through when I felt troubled. There seemed to be some spiritual energy that made communication easier at such times. I soon understood he wanted us to correspond on a regular basis. I learned how to tune those energies toward his frequencies in order to be in touch more readily. In our letters, we discussed our relationship and the meanings of both this life and the afterlife.

My goal is not to prove the truth of life after death or communication from the deceased. I simply want to speak of what has helped me. Mine is a love story, a self-help book, a journal, and through an introduction to metaphysical concepts, a glimpse into the greater mysteries of existence.

After selling most of our possessions, I left Hawaii to begin a nine-month pilgrimage of healing, to find peace and joy again. I visited Florida, Georgia, and Virginia, and I traveled extensively in Europe (Amsterdam, Italy, Switzerland, Germany and Greece). Each place had a part in my recovery. I worked with a Philippine psychic surgeon. I traveled far into the realms of the spirit world and reconnected with my husband. I awoke my passion for life and cleared out unconscious negative thought patterns. I learned the teaching power of plants, sacred rituals and trance dance. I experienced days of soul hunting to call back my power. On the Island of Corfu, I began to write the letters to Rock, and there I danced with my soul for five days, feeling full of light, bliss, and overflowing joy. My pilgrimage ended; I had found my way home to self.

I am a private person, so there is much that hasn't been easy for me to disclose. Some of the letters have no closure because I didn't finish them.

May reading my story in some way benefit you and awaken you to the truth of life.

Blessings,
Loryn "Solana" Walton

Part One

Letters from the Greek Islands

Searching for Your Spirit

June 2, 1996

My beloved Rock,

I sensed from the beginning I would need to write it all down at some time and now that I just finished a powerful, week-long healing retreat, I am ready. I have one week left on this mystical Greek Island of Corfu filled with ancient groves of olive trees. Being able to express myself to you is a precious gift, and being in touch with you makes me feel you're with me now. I sense that you're reading over my shoulder and that you can feel my love and gratitude.

Your spirit left your body on July 21, 1995, a hot and sunny Friday afternoon, only twenty-one days after we were married.

I was surprised when Mrs. Miller called me at the gallery. How did she know I worked there? She told me you had fallen or passed out and they had called an ambulance. I said I would come right away.

I was the only one in the gallery and had to find someone to watch the place. Although my impulse was to go to you immediately, I couldn't leave over a million dollars worth of art unattended. Everyone else was in a meeting. I finally found someone and took off.

The drive was traumatic. I had no idea what was happening, and I was very scared. I wanted to drive extremely fast and pass every car on the road through town, but I had to crawl when I wanted to run. I wanted to honk the horn and flash my lights and clear everybody out of my way. Sometimes we judge people when they drive crazily. I realized then how we never really know what is going on in other people's minds.

I was unsure just where to go. The turn-off to the hospital was coming up soon, so I stopped at the Aloha Cafe and called Mrs. Miller. No answer. Maybe everyone was outside. I continued for another long fifteen minutes to her house. I prayed hard for God to keep you safe. It gave me strength as I drove. I kept remembering a recent dream about you, the one we had discussed. I hadn't understood it, but its answer was to keep you in the light. I prayed out loud and spoke to God, again begging him to watch over you while I endured an eternity of trying to reach you.

When I arrived Mrs. Miller said they had taken you to the hospital. I asked the dreaded question: "Is he alive?" She didn't know, and I perceived the depth of her concern. Back to the hospital I went, still praying. Honey, I was awfully scared. It was so hard to think you might be dead. I tried not to let myself believe it possible.

I followed signs for the emergency room of our small hospital. There were no parking spaces. How absurd; I needed to be with you, so I parked illegally.

I ran inside and said I was looking for Rock Walton, that I was his wife. "Wife." That word was so dear to me. Here in the hospital it seemed sacred. Just three weeks ago we had our beautiful private ceremony with dolphins surrounding our boat in Kealekekua Bay. They added joy to our special day. After living together for two years we committed ourselves to being husband and wife. You were someone I could trust to stay by my side, someone I wanted in my life.

"Sit down out in the waiting room, and the doctor will be with you shortly," the receptionist said. I obeyed, thinking, these people are crazy. They want me to sit there, and wait patiently. Then, in the hallway, I saw your co-worker, Walt. We touched hands, and I prayed out loud with him. That wasn't something I would normally have done, but it helped keep me sane. A woman in green hospital clothes appeared. I had no idea what was happening, and no one would tell me until I asked the dreaded question, "Is he dead or alive?" She hesitated a moment before saying quite slowly that you were dead.

I went into shock. I'm not really sure how it happened, but I stormed through the door and past the emergency-room desk, where they wouldn't let me pass before, to find you. "Stop her!" someone yelled out. Three men started toward me and then for some reason let me alone. Looking back, it was as if some benevolent force was protecting me. There were two curtained rooms, and I knew you were in one of them.

I found you. Finally I found you! They were still trying to pump your heart to bring you back. I was furious that the woman told me you were dead, when these people were still trying to revive you. I felt I needed just to touch your body. I had to do my best to contact your spirit wherever it was, plead with you to come back into your body, and to plead with God not to let you die.

The doctor said no; I had to get out, and I could not touch you. He spoke with a tone of voice that was soft and gentle as if he cared. But inside I felt he was as cold as ice and had no feelings. At that moment, I truthfully disliked him. Then a woman came and said it would be okay, and I could touch your feet for a minute and do whatever I needed to do. Somehow, she knew that perhaps my touch could accomplish more than what their machines were doing. She was an angel.

It felt so much better to have found you. There were five people in there, but I spoke to you, not caring what anybody thought. I just kept saying, "Please, Rock, come back to me." Your feet were very cold, and I could feel your spirit was no longer in your body. At some level I was sending my consciousness out searching for your spirit in the cosmos to see if I could find you and bring you back. I didn't feel your spirit in the room.

The "ice doctor" ordered me back to the reception area,

but I refused to go.

"I will sit right here outside his room. As long as you're still working on him I need to stay close and keep praying," I said. They let me stay for a while and again tried to oust me. I was creating problems because now the other people wanted to be in with their loved one.

It's as if I can sense you saying, "That's my Bee," still lovingly calling me by your nickname for me. You always sort of giggled when I was forceful with people. Even if you looked a bit concerned. You seemed to respect me when I entered a mode of real strength. I can feel you now remembering it was senseless for anyone to argue with me when I had made a decision. How exasperated you often got at my "stubbornness," as you called it!

Yes, it was my space. If they wanted me to leave they would have to pick me up and carry me out; I needed to be near you and listen to what the doctors were doing. I could hear them moving, pumping your heart and counting.

The sounds stopped...someone came to me...everything blurred. From somewhere came those familiar words about sitting down in another room and the doctor would be with me... It was quite irritating. I'm not sure in what order things happened. There by my side, being supportive was Angelica, the angel woman who let me touch your feet. A police officer interviewed me. I could feel he was uncomfortable at having to get information from me and of course I didn't make it much easier. There was anger in my voice when I had to answer ridiculous questions. I now understand that the anger was a defense to cover my pain. I do remember thinking, my husband just died and you want to ask me if I know his social security number!

It seemed there was some idea his death needed investigating: it wasn't normal for a young, healthy looking man of thirty-three just to drop dead. "Did you have AIDS or a drug problem?" he asked. I did tell them you'd gotten sick the night before and we thought it was the fish. God, honey, I even feared you had died of food poisoning, and I was the one who had bought it. The officer said an autopsy would determine the cause of death.

Then it was time for the doctor. He was certainly not like the ones we used to watch on "ER," where they at least seemed to have a heart. It was difficult for me to listen to him. He knew the right words and the right tone of voice, but his feelings were shut down. It was as if he were acting, and it made me angry.

Angelica kept asking me if there was someone I wanted to call. Did I have any relatives on the island? I didn't. All of them were far away on the East Coast of the United States, which seemed a world away.

Mrs. Miller called, the first to whom I pronounced the words, "Rock is dead." I couldn't even believe what I heard myself saying. She was genuinely empathetic and very supportive. I had an urge to call my manager, Ed, at the gallery in order to find his wife. Sharon was the closest friend I had on the island, and Angelica kept telling me I shouldn't be alone. So once again I had to say, "Rock is dead." Ed started to cry and I was so touched. My boss—and our friend, wept at your loss, not only for me but also for himself.

In a short time, you and he established a deep connection. You both had a similar gentleness of soul and enjoyed getting to know each other. You especially liked going fishing with him. When he and his family came over for the day, they had come to see our animals-the new colt, our black puppy, and our famous, good-natured Rotweiller-Doberman mix, Rufus.

I asked Ed to find Sharon for find me. While on the phone,

I heard the doctor telling someone to make me get off. It was on his desk. I was fed up with that insensitive man.

"Okay, I am off your phone," I shouted. "Are you happy now?"

The whole room became still. All attention focused on our interchange. He certainly seemed surprised. I don't think he realized I had heard his command. I could sense from their reaction that his attitude had also been affecting them. Ten people all stopped, watching and listening. Then the doctor went into his 'play act' of the right words in the right tone. I couldn't wait to get out of that hospital.

Looking back, I understand why a doctor might choose to cut off his feelings. Being emotional could interfere with quickly making a correct decision. He was attempting to make an effort to seem caring. What an empty life to live, only in the world of the mind. What a challenge to be caring, yet still able to make critical decisions. We all have to find the balance between feelings, mind, and spirit.

Angelica said there was more paperwork to be done upstairs. They were moving you into a small private room, and if I wanted to be alone with you, this was the time to do it.

Finally! I had my wish, but I could sense they were keeping an eye on me from outside. Now there we were, you and I. Together, alone. In that room I went through a lot with you.

It is now 4:40 a.m. and I will continue at another time. It's almost as if I have to prepare myself to go through the next part again. I love you dearly and feel you with me often, especially now as I write. It is so good to be aware of your closeness. Perhaps we'll fly together tonight in my dreams.

I promise to write again soon, probably tomorrow.

Your loving wife - Loryn

Broken Promise

June 2

Hello again, beloved,

I had five hours of sleep, a good Greek omelet for breakfast, and I went shopping. The roads here are small cobblestone, hilly, streets with all sorts of small mom and pop stores tucked away in the corners, mixed in with little cafes. I bought more stationary, orange juice, and to be good to myself, a beautiful pair of white Greek sandals with gold strands woven into them. After climbing my way up all the stairs and finding my way through the maze of back alleys, I found my way back to this small inexpensive room I rented from an old Greek woman who lives downstairs. Now I am with you again.

I think there's some resistance to going through the "room scene" again. I felt I was with you the whole night, discussing many things in my dreams. Now back to the hospital. Your sheet-covered, 5'11", 206-pound body lay there on the bed. Your beautiful brown hair (that I asked you to grow long) was back in a ponytail. Your beard and mustache helped to cover your white face. In a bag nearby were your work clothes and the new boots we had just bought together. I wanted nothing to do with the finality that bag represented.

When I touched your hand, it was so cold. I could feel you weren't inside your body. Your spirit always kept your body warm, a warmth you so often shared with me.

Now I could call you the name I used to when we were alone. "Bear," the name Bear, because you were big and brown, but also soft and cuddly like a Teddy Bear. We used to take time out of the day to have cuddle breaks. I melted into your arms, feeling so loved and protected. But here was this body, cold and empty. "BEAR!" I called out. At last I broke down and sobbed, still hoping we would both wake up and be together again. I just couldn't believe this was possible. "Bear, Why, Why?" I cried. I gave out a mournful wail that I'm sure echoed up and down the hall.

All of a sudden I was furious with you for leaving me. I remember reading that anger is one of the natural phases people go through after someone dies. What amazed me was how I kept experiencing all these aspects of myself. At some points, I was totally into the despair and at other points I was witnessing myself and amazed to see myself in such a state of being.

I reminded you of our promise that if we go, we would go together so neither one of us would have to live through the death of the other. Neither one of us was afraid of death. We felt it was just going to a place no different than the places we used to travel to together in our meditations. But we did have a fear of being left without the other and there I was. You were gone, and I was left to have to deal with it. It seems reasonable enough to feel angry.

Then I had an overwhelming feeling, I wanted to just be with you wherever you were. If there was something in the room that would have helped me to end my life quickly, I might have done it. Not because I wanted to end my life, but because I really just wanted to be with you. In fact, this thought had passed through my mind many times...

June 3

So, my dear,

I can see I didn't close the last letter. It has been on my mind a lot. It has been quite challenging going through the "room scene" again.

I guess Angelica also felt I'd had enough. She led me out of your room and mentioned something about taking care of some funeral arrangements. I followed Angelica upstairs and she turned me over to another gentle, caring woman, Carol.

Carol asked me what kind of arrangements I wanted to make and what funeral home I wanted to use. She proceeded to tell me the differences in the few funeral homes, including one, which tended to be less expensive. I told her you wanted to be cremated. I knew you wanted the same thing you had done for your dad just a few years ago. She said it would be around $1,000. I told her I didn't even have $100. In the back of my mind I couldn't believe I had to go through all of this. Here I am, my husband just died and they want me to start shopping for funeral arrangements, plus come up with money I didn't have. It seemed too much to have to handle at one time.

Carol told me of an organization that grants money in such cases and proceeded to assist me in filling out their application. It seems so crazy the way our society is set up, that we have to pay so much money to bury our dead.

Then I hear over the loudspeaker, a page for the owner of a blue Honda Civic. I knew they would search me out sooner or later. So excuse me, my husband just died. Heaven forbid someone's car is parked in a different parking lot. What is the world coming to? It was the perfect excuse to get out quickly.

Walt found me to tell me I needed to move my car. Carol, knowing I was ready to leave, made an appointment for me to meet with the funeral director right down the road (how convenient), but I would have to wait 15 minutes before she arrived. Do Do's funeral home. I used to laugh at the name when I drove past. I never imagined I would one day be using them.

Walt walked me to my car. He was very supportive and he mentioned how he also had been through a similar experience. I didn't say anything but I remembered you had told me his wife had also died unexpectedly. I was touched by him sharing that with me.

He offered to drive me home or follow me home and I strongly refused. Then he offered to find a way to bring your work truck back home. I thought that would be a good idea and thanked him for taking care of it.

I headed on down the hill. I didn't want to just sit there and wait at the funeral home — but something told me I should really take care of it now. As I was sitting out front, I saw Sharon. She was just about to turn up the street to the hospital. I yelled out to her and she pulled into the parking area. She ran up to me and really hugged me and we both cried. I had been in a sort of numbness up until then, trying to get through all the "red tape."

Here, finally, was a nurturing energy I knew and trusted

and a heart that understood my pain. I was so glad she was there.

Bear, I am going to take a cigarette break now. All this has brought up many tears for me, and you know how every once in a while I will smoke when I am feeling emotionally upset. I love you dearly and feel you with me.

Until later-Loryn

Power of Gratitude

June 4

My dear beloved Rock,

I am once again drawn to this paper to be in communication with you. As I write, I look up to see your beautiful smiling face, looking at me with those brown eyes I so loved to look into. Every time I look at your photo, my heart just fills with all the love we created and are still creating. We asked for this you know. Remember how almost daily we prayed to God to give us the true meaning of love and allow that love bring us closer to divine love. I remember, at times, I would sense that this might look differently than I expected. Regardless, we were both sincere in our request. We both had a deep love for God and a desire to experience the

21

Divine.

I believe I am now experiencing this with you. I love you and accept you, not thinking you should be different than you are or do anything different. I respect your space, knowing you have your own path and it may or may not be with me. Our relationship is so peaceful, joyful and sometimes still exciting. There is a real feeling of togetherness that can't be threatened or taken away. I know, Bear, that you watch over me and, at times, guide me.

I am able to maintain this attitude for the most part, even though it has taken me a while to get here. Sometimes, on emotionally low days, I do forget.

I think it's also fun when I intuitively receive a suggestion from you about how to handle certain situations in my present relationship. You gently remind me of some of the same patterns I had with you. That's the love we are experiencing— loving the person so much that you can support that person to continue to experience love with someone other than yourself. I do admit it certainly is a unique situation to be having a relationship here on earth and working on my relationship there with you in the spirit world. I am sure I will write to you more on this subject later.

I really appreciate your guidance, love and support. I appreciate all the love and support you gave to me while you were here on the planet. I am grateful to have experienced such a wonderful love with you even if it was for just a short time. The gifts you have given me, and the gifts that God has given me through you, have been tremendous.

Oh, my sweet Bear, I can feel your love enfold me as I write these words. You've always been able to touch my heart in such a sweet, soft way.

Your love and acceptance has always been such a healing for me. You loved things about me that I had judged as wrong. Your love healed me in so many ways and it still does.

I feel your energy now, so gentle, soft and tingling. I can hear you calling, "Bee."

Remember the song we made up, "The Bee and the Bear, and the Bear and the Bee," (we just sang those words over and over). I loved singing that song with you. It was so much fun.

I had a lot of fun with you, especially going out on the boat fishing and watching the dolphins. I loved it when we saw the whales in the winter. It's funny, at that time we were sure we would have a lot more whale watching seasons together.

While here in Greece, I've been seeing the full moon reflect on the Mediterranean Sea. I often think of all the times we went out on the boat overnight and watched the moon over the water. We did create some real magical times with each other. We loved being with each other. The fact that we both remembered to be grateful for each other, I feel, is one of the secrets that made our relationship so wonderful.

It really made a difference after we created the habit of saying thank you to God, almost every night that we were in each other's life. There is something about hearing you say out loud to God, "Thank you God for Loryn being in my life, or thank you God for my Bee." It created even a deeper love for you, and a deep sense of gratitude for you being in my life.

Actually, my Bear, sweet, sweet Bear, I still am grateful you're in my life. How empty people must feel that really believe there is no after life. I felt really empty there for a while and I <u>do</u> believe in an after life.

For me, it was like you flew unexpectedly to a foreign

country and I, or we, had to discover how to use these foreign communication systems. I'm not sure what it was like for you, although I sense you also were trying to get through to me. Actually you did get through to me.

I recall the first night I slept alone without you. I dreaded going into that large king-size bed, knowing once again I would have to really deal with you not being there.

Sharon was in the house with me. Her caring energy gently supported me in the background as I called people for hours that night. I kept having to say those words over and over again, "Rock had a heart attack and died." To some people, like some of your customers I had to first tell them we were just married and then tell them you died. Somehow it was very helpful to keep letting it out. I don't know how many people I called or how late it was at night, but I finally did it. I got into the bed and just cried and cried. Crying out to God, asking him, "Why?"

I need to take a break now from all this. I am going to sleep now, Bear. I love you dearly, and hope to join you this evening in my dreams.

Love, your Bee, Loryn

Higher Purpose

June 4

Hello, beloved,

Again last night, I had to stop writing as the tears streamed down my face while I remembered the "hospital scene."

I thought of you today as I sat by the crystal clear, turquoise water watching the men fishing from the land. On my way to the airport, I walked by all the boats at the harbor remembering our love of boats and our dreams of sailing these Greek islands together.

Now, as I fly back to the Athens airport, I will go back to the "bed scene." First after climbing into bed I remember crying out for help and asking the angels to be with me. I was feeling such extreme emptiness in my heart. I called out for some relief from this depth of pain piercing my heart. I immediately felt a loving energy come and comfort me. It was as if a huge wing of love came and enveloped me until I finally fell asleep.

I did sense you trying to calm me down later throughout the night. You always had a way of knowing how to calm me down when I became real emotional. I could sense you saying, "Feel our love, feel our love, then you can feel our connection." I would calm down and feel the love we have and I could sense you with me and feel comforted. I would feel a warm, tingling feeling in my heart. Then I would remember what happened and lose it again.

I do remember, though, making a choice on how I was going to choose to handle this mentally. It was a very strong and strange experience. Hanging from the ceiling, to the left side of the bed, were many different thought patterns. And I had to contemplate all of them and choose one. Some of them were:

It could have been prevented.

I could have done something different.

You could have done something different.

We could have gone earlier to the doctor.

We could have gone to another doctor.

If only the doctor had done tests when you told him you

had chest pains.

It was just your time to go.

Maybe you had the choice to come back and you chose

not to.

These thoughts, plus more, seemed to be hanging in the air for me to choose from. The one I chose was, "It was just your time to move on and God in her/his/its Divine Wisdom had a higher purpose, that obviously I didn't see or understand but had to trust." This thought pattern was the one I had to choose to help me get through it all. To somehow reach for my trust in the Divine and let it hold my hand and say, "It's okay Loryn, everything really is in Divine Order."

It was the one thought that gave me the most strength. It certainly reminded me there was a **Higher Power** and "It" was in charge. That there was both free will and destiny. Your death caused me to surrender to that power and trust deeply. Often times, I think it was a test in my trust of God. How often do I hear of people that lose their faith at times like these. For me it was the opposite. It somehow strengthened my faith.

In the middle of the night I woke up to the words from the Hawaiian wedding song that we sang to each other during our wedding ceremony, "I will love you longer than forever, I do, I do, love you, love you, with all my heart."

I know you were sending me love.., it was so beautiful and so comforting. You were always such a romantic. Then the realization again came to me and the tears once again returned. I had really hoped to wake up and realize that it had been all a dream, meant to teach me a valuable lesson.

I now had to face this first day without you and the things that had to be done. Being on the phone was what seemed to be comforting, just to keep talking about it, getting it out, feeling support from others that also cared for you.

The amount of support from people was tremendous. Nobody in our family had money, yet all of a sudden, your mom and her friend Charlotte came to be with me. Then, my sister, Mari, left her new business and was with me a week, watching over me and helping me take care of practi-

cal matters. My friend, Ba-Bara, came back and performed
the services after just being there three weeks ago to per-
form our wedding ceremony. Then, my youngest sister,
Brenda, came out and supported me through the last month
of selling off things and sending some things back to the
mainland to my sister Mari and her husband's house in
Florida.

I'll tell you, Bear, I was a wreck; my mind was in a fog. It
was very difficult to make decisions. I was grateful I had
people around to watch over me. I kept feeling apologetic,
because I seemed to be handling things less efficiently than
I usually did. It was like being under the influence of alco-
hol, without being drunk.

I did feel when you communicated to me how wonderful
you were feeling, how you had realized you never knew the
magnificence of who you were. I always could see what a
beautiful spirit you were.

It was just at that time, I really couldn't share in your
joy. I sensed you telling me there wasn't really a problem.
You would wait for me and we would soon be together again.
I remember arguing back to you. Oh yeah, it's no problem
for you. You have no sense of time. What may seem like

moments to you would feel like eons for me. You were up there "flying around" and I was here having to take care of a mess. It's funny to think I could even be mad at you.

Also, I remember sensing that you wanted me still to do the healing we had planned to do in a few days. You wanted to experience healing with me from your new sense of self. I told you that you were nuts and there was no way I could just forget all that happened and focus on being a channel of healing, although later on I did contemplate it. How bizarre that just last month we were doing healings on our wedding night and this month you wanted to do them, but with you working from the other side. It actually would have been beautiful if I could have managed it. What ended up happening was that your funeral services were held that night and some of the people came to that.

You sure did surprise a lot of people. Just within three weeks we had met about fifty new people through the firewalk, sweat lodge, and the energy healing night. They were all shocked how one minute you had become a new friend to them, and the next minute you were gone. It really seems to me that those last three weeks of your life were like a huge, long going away party. And how strange it seemed that you had reconnected shortly with some old friends that had ended up being a good-bye for you.

I could sense that it was difficult for you to see me so distraught. You wanted me to share your joy in your new-found freedom and the connection of our love. And instead, I went into the sadness of losing you. I still wonder today if it's possible for any human being to lose someone dear to them, and not feel sad because their loved one is physically gone.

Well, I'm landing in Athens now so I've got to go. Until later my love...

Sadness

June 5

Hello again, honey,

Well, last night was somewhat challenging- arriving in a large foreign city late at night and having a taxi driver take me to a Greek hotel. I stayed in Athens to make my connecting flight today to the USA more convenient. I am sure spoiled by the luxury of America. I was nervous seeing the inadequate locks on the door. In America we have all of these triple locks so you know no one will walk in on you, although maybe there you need them and here you don't. I consciously called on you last night to protect me. You reminded me I was safe, and I called upon all of my soul and moved into the blissful state that I feel with you and my soul. I still struggled moving in and out of feeling safe and feeling scared.

Sadness is definitely something I learned about. I feel as if I entered a semester of Sadness 101 in Earth University, or maybe it's more like an advanced course in sadness.

It seemed like this was a cycle of my life to experience sadness. I felt we as human beings are meant to experience all ranges of human emotions. It's like a soul experience. In some way we gain knowledge through these experiences. I had resisted crying and sadness much in my life because I had quite often felt it was wrong. How often do we try to get children and friends to stop crying? Often it is because we don't want to feel their sadness.

I still felt this. It had been very difficult for those around me to hear me cry so deeply, and so someone had always come over with loving arms to comfort me. I felt they didn't want me to cry. So I decided to stop crying around them and then I felt myself blocked.

I remember I went into the shower, and finally alone, I started to cry. I was really sobbing. I sensed you there with me. I know it was hard for you to see me this way.

I could control the sobbing but not the tears. Tears were

uncontrollably in my eyes quite often when I was speaking to people. They were just coming out at a slower pace.

I will continue more with the sadness lesson later today while I am on the plane. I must get ready now for my flight back to the good old USA.

Later, love.

June 5

Dear Bear,

So...the lessons of sadness.

First there was the acceptance of myself. I had to change my viewpoint on crying in front of others, from one of weakness to just a natural, necessary human expression. I also saw how it touched others to feel deeper.

That is what the sadness did for me. It allowed me to feel a depth of myself I had never experienced before. When I stood back and witnessed myself I was amazed at my depth of feeling. I don't know why, somehow, we have the viewpoint sadness is to be avoided. If we took away the judgment on it, sadness can be an incredible experience. And somehow it made me even more aware of the love I felt for you.

I was experiencing many different aspects of myself, one that was shocked by the traumatic experience. There was the witness that could calmly watch myself react so deeply and be amazed by the drama of the whole situation. Then, also, my normal, positive personality came out. It had to; it was such a part of me.

The awareness of a part of myself, witnessing myself was a phenomenal experience. It was as if I was tapping into a greater aspect of myself and I was having simultaneous experiences of being emotionally involved and emotionally detached. The witness was able to watch, but had no viewpoint of labeling the experience good or bad. It just was!

I know people with me thought how good I was handling things because I seemed in a good state of mind. But deep inside I was very fragile. I became extremely sensitive to other people's feelings and any type of harshness. It's like any barriers I might have created to deal with harshness had dropped away. I seemed to be in the same vulnerable state as I was when I was a child.

It was as if a tornado had come and wiped out the house I lived in (the energy field around me). Now I had to totally rebuild my house, brick by brick, with more conscious energy. I had no idea how it was going to happen, especially on a financial level with only $25 in my pocket and a lot of bills to be paid.

There was so much support from so many people. People started sending me cards with money in them. I was so grateful. It helped one part of me to relax. And our generous landlord told me not to worry about paying the rent. Your friend Mike offered to pay the funeral arrangements and my work offered to pay the phone bill, which was large, due to all the long-distance calls.

Your friend Stan came and offered to keep your landscape business going with Walt working with him, which also helped bring money in. Since Stan decided to work the business I knew I would have to manage it. It kept me busy and kept my mind occupied which was helpful.

It was really like a huge vacuum. All that I lost seemed to create a void that began being filled with new and different energies. Again, as I stood back and watched, I could see the universe was really at work taking care of things.

Through it all, I kept feeling a closer connection to God.

I was glad your mom was with me and really grateful I had gotten to know her just two months before when she visited us. It was like she and I were moving through things together making whatever decisions that had to be made about whatever.

It was quite strange having to arrange a service for you. We really had no idea what we were going to do. More and more people asked us if we were going to have a service.

Just a month ago I was being educated on all the things that needed to be done to get married, and now a short time later, I'm learning about funeral services. It still all seemed so bizarre to me.

Things came together with the help of many people and a true aloha spirit. At first we had a private boat ride to throw the ashes into the sea. There were seven of us. Your friend Paul was very generous to offer to take us out on his fifty-foot boat. Your other friend, Astral had offered first, but Paul's boat just fit us all more comfortably and had a bathroom. In fact, because two people had offered their boats and Astral had already put his in the water, I ended up in quite a predicament. I certainly didn't want to hurt Astrals' feelings. I will always be grateful for Astral giving up the pride of carrying your ashes out to sea.

We picked up the ashes from the funeral home. In my mind I had visualized light black ashes like those that are left after a wood fire. Instead the box was very heavy. It must have been those extra ten pounds you had gained. It was so strange to think what was left of your body was in this brown, rectangular shaped, plastic box.

The weather was beautiful as we boarded the boat. It was hard to stay in a solemn mood. I was on a beautiful boat, on the Hawaiian water, with great weather and people that cared for you. Your dad's old friend, Jeremy, was making jokes, as usual, trying to keep spirits up. He joked about not remembering the exact coordinates of where they put your dad's ashes saying this time they would pay closer attention for sake of the next one to go.

Well my dear, I'm about to land in the New York airport. Until later...

Part Two

Letters from the Blue Ridge Mountains

Letting Go

June 6

Hello, beloved,

I'm back in the USA visiting one of my old hometowns. I am enjoying the North Georgia wooded landscape. My friend here has a beautiful three-bedroom house tucked away in the woods with lots of great walking trails and rafting streams. There is also a wonderful room that I use for trance dancing, since there are few neighbors to hear the drumbeats of the music.

It has been a joy traveling around together with you. It had been something I had always wanted to do. We talked about the exotic places we would visit. And now you're traveling all over with me, just a little differently than expected, I assumed you would have traveled with a physical body. Never the less, I am so glad I know you're with me.

I felt very lost for a while. I had misunderstood what it meant to release the dead. I had believed in the concept, that when one dies, we should let them go and not pull them down to the earth with our thoughts. I had consciously made an effort to let you go in a ceremony where myself and five other women communicated with you three months before. I had actually blocked out your presence. I thought maybe I was interfering with your life by continuing to communicate with you. I consciously chose to let our relationship go because of this concept. I need to be more discerning with what concepts I blindly believe, especially since I was getting the sense that my own inner guidance was telling me differently.

I had a realization of a deeper truth during my travels through Europe this year. In March, while in Italy, I had a powerful experience during one of my classes. It was a ten-day workshop that focused on shattering all past concepts and thoughts that stopped us from experiencing the Oneness of all that there is and live in the present. It dealt with issues with our parents, with fear, of truly communicating to people what we are thinking of them, and allowing them to truly communicate to us, and issues of needing approval, etc. It was very intense and powerful, including the fact I was the only American student with about thirty Italians and I didn't know how to speak Italian.

It was an uncomfortable situation not being able to talk to many people but I was very determined to do what I had to do to heal myself and have a sense of being back on track with my life.

Appropriately while there, we were given the opportunity to attend the funeral of someone we were all acquainted with and the timing was used to bring up our feelings and fears of death. When I went up to the coffin I surprisingly sobbed. Somewhere inside me I knew I was not just feeling the sadness of this friends' death but it was touching again that place inside me that was still dealing with your death.

Later on that evening we all did a trance dance ceremony as both a prayer and a healing. We called in the wisdom of the soul for insight into the meaning of death and help to heal from the sense of loss. As I was dealing with my issues around death you came into my mind. I opened up to you and felt your presence. I felt you communicate that it would actually benefit both of us if we maintained some level of connection. I was so happy to be able to feel you again and know it was okay.

I then realized that I had misunderstood what it meant to release the dead. The concept has some truth that we need to release the <u>attachment</u> to our loved ones, but we do not need to close off the feelings of love. It was helpful to know you were still with me helping me adjust to your new form and my new way of life. Your presence was such an important part of my adjustment.

Well, dear, I must go until tomorrow.

Much love,

Loryn

Sacrifice of Death

June 7

Hello, my beloved Rock,

I have just recently been reminded that we have a one-year wedding anniversary coming up in three weeks. Perhaps that was why I was drawn to write to you at this time. It also means that we have a one year anniversary of your death approaching. It amazes me to think it's been almost one year since you physically left your body. The whole thing still seems like a dream I had.

My life has changed so much this year, which I suppose reflects how much I've changed. The changes I know have resulted from the gifts you have given me from your death. There are so many changes and experiences I am grateful for. You know I believe before we come to earth we choose our plan for our life. We choose major events that will assist us in our evolution. Perhaps we had made the agreement that at the height of our love, you would die suddenly so I would receive the maximum opportunity for accelerated growth. A friend of mind said recently, "It's as if they sacrifice their lives for us when they die."

Choosing Joy

June 8

Hello, dear one,

Once again I have the pleasure of being in communication with you. One thing I notice is that during challenging times, I miss you the most. Times when it seems life is cruel. That is when I want to be back in the protection of your arms again, although I do realize that I am meant to gain strength through these situations.

I've also noticed how so many people judge because they do not understand. Even I sometimes forget that everyone is on their own path and we really have no idea what that path is. So we say, "Oh that is wrong." But in truth, there really is no right or wrong, everything just is what it is.

I remember how many people judged the way we chose to be in our relationship as wrong, because we chose to keep to ourselves rather then go out and socialize a lot, (especially many of your old partying friends). I understand that they missed your company. And I certainly don't blame them for that. But what they didn't realize was what it was like to have what we had. Plus, you also wanted to stop drinking. Sometimes we have to separate ourselves from patterns of the past and totally jump into being a new way. No one realized that we would only have two years together. I felt intuitively that what we were doing was right for us and I dealt with the judgments from those that didn't understand.

After your death I was able to heal those relationships, because now they understood why. I was grateful for the healing and grateful for their support and understanding. And it was good to share stories with those that also had loved you.

More and more as I continue to listen to my inner guidance I seem to have to deal with other's judgments and also with disappointing others. It's never easy disappointing others, but I've learned that my inner voice is always to be trusted to put me where it is best for me to be. And that is what I use as my strength.

Of course, at times, this had also happened within our relationship. There were times when you were really hurt by what I felt I had to do. Remember when we discussed having a child. You really wanted to have a son, I believed to re-create the relationship you had with your dad. But I felt we should wait so that we had time to create a firm enough bond between us that would hold us together during the challenges of raising a child. Plus, we had so little money. Thus, I had agreed to have a child with you one year after our marriage. This would also give us some time to enjoy our time together alone as husband and wife. I remember the night we met. You asked me to marry you and have your child. You had said you sensed I was the woman you wanted to raise a child with. Often times we would imagine the joys of parenthood together. I also felt you were a man I would trust to raise a child with me.

I have a sense that I made an agreement with a soul friend or friends that I would only bring them into this world if I felt comfortable with the conditions around me. What scared me most about our condition was the lack of money. I felt if I had a child I would want to give them so much and how frustrated I would feel if I couldn't. Oh, I know between the both of us the child would get plenty of love, which is most important, but it is also nice to have the material comforts of life.

I admit I am glad I followed my feelings, even though it caused you great sadness. One day when I was speaking to a friend of mine about it, I cried deeply only then realizing how much it hurt to have you not understand and be disappointed. I hope now you can understand. Even though I know there would have been blessings to have your child with me now, as a memory of our love, we would be going through many hardships getting along in the material world. I've been very careful in my decisions for childbearing, not to end up a single mother. I honor all women that are choosing that path, but I've known it was not a path I wanted to take.

I think respect is a word that would help me to realize not to judge. I feel that as I begin to respect more the yearnings of my own soul and listen to that voice, I will also realize the importance of respecting other people's choices. I see how judgment, control, and domination can be replaced with respect. It seems to start with a respect for my own self and my particular soul path, and then move to others, including respect for the earth. I can see how once I live in total respect for my Self, and all aspects of that Self it will just flow out into having respect for all life.

As I get deeper in touch with my soul, I accept all things as myself and I feel the connection with all. This also is a gift your death has given me— the gift of reconnecting with my soul. Your death caused me to make choices differently than I had before.

The sadness was so deep. The choice was to stay in the sadness, which wasn't very motivating, or to reach for joy which gave me lots more energy and light. It was as if I chose to create joy out of necessity. In the past I didn't make decisions based on joy, because I felt it wasn't as great an accomplishment as something I worked hard for. Working hard was greater than choosing joy. Then joy became a real need. Creating joy is part of our purpose in this life because it brings us into a closer connection with the Divine.

Dancing and swimming are things that have always been very joyful to me. Remember the night we met. We danced till we were the only ones on the dance floor. But it didn't matter. We were so entranced with each other.

I recall the time I put on Gabrielle Roth's music and we danced the five rhythms together. It all happened so spontaneously and I was absolutely overjoyed to be dancing with you. Then there was that time in our new house you put on Billy Idol and we just started dancing. It was so much fun. And then, of course our last dance together was the night of our wedding. I really wanted to dance on our wedding night, so after the healings I totally shifted the energy and put on Billy Idol to dance to. I remember you couldn't believe I would have the nerve to do this. After all, everyone was wearing white and in a holy sacred energy, and I switched it to some rock and roll to dance to. I did it with the intention that spirituality could be holy, quiet and sacred but we could also be loud, wild and free and have fun and be spiritual. Now I am glad to have done it.

After your death, I felt more motivated to find a way to bring the joy of dance more into my life. I started to search for music that moved me because that had been part of the problem. I didn't find music that kept me dancing.

I started to buy books on dancing, looked into dance therapy training, and started experimenting with different music. And finally one day I found it, *Trance Dance* by Frank

Natale. This was the answer to my quest. But the rest of this story I must save for another time for I must go for now.

Until tomorrow dear. Much love and blessings to you and thank you for spending this time with me.

Sensitivity

June 9

Dear Bear,

As I lay here feeling the insensitivity of the world, I feel sad and think once again of our love. That feeling that seems to make the world alive again. Your devoted love to me makes me feel cared for. I realize that this love is also the same love that is God, Goddess, the energy of the Oneness that we all are. God or the Universe has put you on my path to be a reflection of that love.

Yes, it is true there were times we were insensitive to each other's feelings, but now you're where you are and I can feel your total sensitivity. We have even a greater relationship now than when you were physically here. How wonderful to have a model for a good relationship. It is such a blessing and a gift to feel your love and support for me always. No matter how I am, you still feel love for me. And yes, so it is the same with God's love. It is always there loving me and supporting me no matter how I am.

I do not know if it is really possible for any human being to totally love unconditionally. If we try to rely on that kind of love here, it leads to disappointment. I'm not sure if this is a faulty thought pattern or a truth. I suppose for now it is a truth. I suppose there is the possibility of humans being like that. And if there are, perhaps they are rare and considered saints.

Do you think I have that capability, Bear? I feel that you do believe that I could achieve that state. Is that a state I desire to achieve?

Surprise Communication

June 10

Dear Bear,

Once again, dear one, during my troubled times, I am comforted by your presence, love and understanding. (As I was writing I could sense Rock communicating to me and I wrote down his words)

> *You are a goddess*
> *As beautiful and wild as the sea,*
> *A woman who deserves to be honored*
> *Adored, protected, and cared for.*

You are as strong as the stormy seas

That can turn over huge ships

And as fragile as the water of the gentle seas.

You say that you could see the magnificence of who I

was.

Well, I could see the magnificence of your beauty

And of your heart.

Now, dear one, I see you brighter

Than I did while on earth.

If you really knew the power of who you are,

Your life would be totally different.

It would be filled with the love,

Abundance, joy and peace that you desire,

Because it is who you really are........

*   *   *

I can see now where some of our ways of manifesting

could have been improved upon. One thing we really

had going for us was that we both wanted the same

thing. Our thoughts were highly focused at those times

when we were working our magic, creating the life we yearned for together.

These thoughts we created are still here; the one with our beautiful house up on the hill in Hawaii overlooking the ocean; with the large property fenced in so Rufus could run free; and raising our children together; feeling and being abundant; working in our garden; going out fishing and sailing; seeing dolphins and whales; and having a beautiful spiritual, sexual relationship. And most important of all was a life filled with love, joy and peace.

That vision has been created here and it's very beautiful to experience. It's a vision that has been added to the world from our love.

It's never a waste of energy to create beautiful, purposeful thoughts even if they don't physically manifest. Everything you think does get created at some level. So, watching your thoughts is important, if you want to consciously know what energy you're putting out into the universe.

Oh, Loryn, I wish I could show you your beauty.

It is challenging at times to be here and watch you go

through your struggles. I so much want to go in and rescue you, and at the same time I can see from here what the value is of your experience. I try as much as I can to get through to you, to guide you. You've always had such a strong mind. I am very grateful now for this moment, when we both are consciously in communication with each other. I am so joyous in our relationship. This love that we now share is the love we prayed to experience.

I know there was something about your touch that was quite pleasurable. It is a fading memory. I suppose you remember more of the pleasure of touch because you still have a body. I also have a memory of what a beautiful expression of a human body you have. As our love grew, it was as if I could see more and more of your inner beauty which shined through your physical beauty even more so. It was a pleasure to set my eyes upon you.

You are truly a goddess of beauty, light and love. See yourself through my eyes and see what I see. Tune into me and look through me.

(Honor)

I get this sense of needing to honor myself, Bear. When I was trance dancing in Greece I had the whole experience of the word honor. It was like I spent hours in this state of being because, trance dancing time seems to expand, like in the dream state. I sensed that experiencing honor would greatly benefit me. I cannot say I have lots of experience with this. When I think of the word what comes up for me is the Ten Commandments. It is said to honor thy mother and father, which include the mother earth. I can sense a need to honor the earth for all it gives us. How she feeds us, gives us air to breath, water to drink, and she allows us to walk and live on her earth body. If I meditate on this I can see how much I can honor this great earth mother, but for myself it was quite an experience to feel I could honor myself. I saw I was honored as a Child of God and part of a great universal family. The memory of the experience has somewhat faded but I remember it was a beautiful experience and one that I wasn't really familiar with.

I am experiencing now not feeling honored. And as I stay with that I can see it is I who is not honoring myself. This is actually a pattern I can now see that has happened before.

A sense of self seems to take time to develop. Perhaps some children get it when they are young. I am not sure I did except maybe when I danced, but even then the dance was done with my brother as my partner. Possibly if I had chosen to continue on dancing after he chose to stop I would have developed one. I do not have a feeling of regret for the decisions I have made in my life except that I chose not to continue dancing. When I was young, right before entering into the first grade around the age of five, I can clearly remember being out in front of the dance studio and my mother giving me the option to continue on even though my brother had decided to stop.

It can be compared to us in a way. I really enjoyed living with you but just because you decided not to physically live here does not mean that is what is best for me to do.

Oh my dear Loryn, my wonderful, beautiful Bee,
I do want you so much to continue to fully live and enjoy your life. To move on- forward- continuing to step towards and into the light. To fully feel the joy of life.

You must honor your soul-self, keep sacred the choice of joy. Trust and feel spirit taking care of you, nurturing you so gently. Know who you are and become it. Be strong, wise and gentle. Hold on to what you know your truth to be. Allow your spirit to nurture you. Open yourself to receive this energy into your being- now....

You are not alone in the world my beloved Loryn. Your world is filled, to be tapped into whenever you choose. Loneliness is an illusion. You're part of such a greater whole. The whole of who you are. Surrendering yourself to spirit to take you and carry you in its arms is a truth. For that is real, the surrendering into spirit. I am with you love and I hold you in my arms and in my heart as you face your shadows of darkness to move into the light. It is all one, both the shadows and the light, the shadow of the tree is from the part that blocks the sunlight. The shadow is neither good or bad, it just is.

My love, allow your heart to rest in mine and feel the safety of true love, the love of God, the energy that connects and holds all together. Let us pray together that you may be lifted out of the cave and onto the moun-tain top to raise above all that is dark in your life. Sur-render into that light. Desire to have love more fully in your life. Remember who you are and move into that self. Do it for me if you must. Reach for the light, reach for the joy, reach for the greatness of your spirit, and of your soul. Take care of your soul. Cherish its gentle-ness, sensitivity and love. Take care to nurture with the love and light that is there for you to tap into.

Hello dear one,

It is sad to see you like this, to know you're feeling so unhappy about your present circumstances. You know what we had and still have is a true gift that we worked on together, it was something we were clear we both wanted. You need to get clear on what you want and to see if it is the same thing those around you want. If it is, keep the vision going. But get clear if you really are going in the same direction in your lives. Keep peace within your heart Loryn. I am with you in spirit always as is the universal God energy. You walk not alone on your path. There are many on this side cheering you on as you walk through the fires of transformation.

Yes honey, to receive honor, you must give honor, for it is in the giving you receive, whether you give it to yourself (soul) or give it to another being. That is how you move the energy through you. You must sometimes put aside your own feelings, honoring them before you put them aside and have the experience of honor. It is always powerful to acknowledge feelings whether they be yours or someone else's. You're so beautiful Bee, you deserve to have honor in your life. It's very close to sacred, it is also very close to respect. These are new values to explore and accept into your life. And remember that as you explore them that others are not necessarily exploring them simultaneously. Be aware that those close to you may not have learned them yet. It might be wise not to expect something from others that you are only beginning to learn yourself.

One thing I remind you of is to BE PATIENT in your teaching of those that are in close relationship with you. Others do not move with the same speed as you. Maybe it would be good to ask for more patience in your life.

You have so many gifts in your life, it would benefit you greatly to keep focused as much as possible on those gifts so they may expand in your life.

Listen to me honey, lift yourself up and fly above the illusion. Yes, sometimes you must dip into it to experience it and imprint the experience upon your soul. It's like as you have traveled to all different countries you check in, have your passport stamped and then check out with your passport again, having experienced the country in the meantime. Bringing back with you things of value. Some you give away and some you keep for yourself. You don't stay in them, you move out of them and look back and find the value. You get in a plane and fly out and above what you were just in.

If you don't like the country you're in you find a way to get out. If you're enjoying the country (or your experience) then you find ways to stay there longer or get the most out of your experience while you're there.

Each emotional experience you have is very valuable to your soul. They allow the opportunity for a tremendous amount of growth in a very short period of time. That's why you/we signed up for time on earth.

The depth and variety of experiences are phenomenal and many are very motivating to evolve.

One of the beautiful things about the nature of earth is its constant changing, its seasons of death, birth, and regeneration. Its wildness and its calmness. It's acceptance and its rejections. Like the Hawaiian volcano goddess, Pele, her beauty is in her fire. Her times of stillness and gentleness and her times of fury are both a magnificence to look upon. She has the power to destroy or wipe out all that is around her at any time. Then, there is always a time to rebuild again. A time to review and look at what was destroyed. To rebuild with a consciousness greater than before.

Life is meant to be experienced at all its levels, and none to be judged as bad or wrong. It's to be experienced, reviewed, and valued by the soul. We gain an enormous amount of strength and wisdom by seeing and accepting the value in all. We then see the things we want to change. And we look at those we are willing or not willing to continue on with in our life.

There is mystery about human life that is meant to be there. Everything is not meant to be understood with the conscious mind. The conscious mind is not always capable of moving into that understanding. Some things are meant to be felt by the heart, and allow the mind to rest by knowing it's okay to accept the mystery of life. If there is a time when the mystery is to be revealed to you, then it will be when the timing is right.

It's like you understand that most of the time you can get in your car and it will start up and drive. But you don't have to totally understand how the car works for you to drive it. The things that are of benefit for you to know about your car are things like, it needs gas, oil, water, a battery, tune ups, oil changes, good tires, windshield wipers, etc. But there are things about the workings of the car that remain a mystery. If you decided to be a mechanic many of the mysteries would be revealed to you, and there would still be more mysteries. One would have to learn about many fields of study in order to really understand the workings of the car, and all the varieties of cars. So the mystery of the car can be honored, as can the mystery of life. It's not always necessary to understand why the experience has happened. It is important to jump in, have the experience, and realize its value.

While trance dancing today I had many experiences related to what you said about seeing the value of what can seem like unpleasant experiences. I saw how my judgments are what interfere with that and how this way of thinking causes insensitivity. I am so aware of the harshness of judgment and am very sensitive to it myself. When it happens to me, after seeing the value, it reminds me to be more sensitive and compassionate for other people's feelings.

When you died I was so aware of the harsh energy of judgment. I was grateful to be reminded and desired to remember to be more sensitive to its energy. More and more I realize we/I have no right to judge anyone because we don't know their path. I saw visions of very difficult times for me when I judged those that were so harshly judging and falsely accusing me. The answer for which I was shown today was to rise above these situations by releasing my judgments. So I prayed for assistance to release them and then consciously released all judgments. I then asked them to be replaced with compassion, sensitivity, and higher knowledge.

I also remembered a powerful spiritual experience I had after a week of meditation at Delphi while dropping off my classmates at the airport. I was walking through the airport and feeling myself glowing and beaming with love and light. I felt as if I were walking on clouds. As I looked at others and smiled I could feel they couldn't help but to feel my energy and smile back. The most profound part that remains strongly in my memory today is when I saw a black man around the age of 60 sleeping in one of the chairs in the airport. I could sense my first reaction would be to think he was a bum living in the streets. I then had a vision where I saw his soul as being this beautiful being that had purposely chosen to live his life in this manner. I could see he was choosing some particular life experiences for his soul. My whole viewpoint changed and I saw him as someone to be honored in his decision rather then judged for his way of living.

To live in this state of being has been my prayer. Recently this prayer has gotten deeper and deeper. In order to see life from this state I know I must live from this place in my heart. I believe I was given this glimpse into this way of living to show me it is possible to live this way. It has not always been clear to me but it is getting clearer and clearer. The more I am at peace with myself, and my life, the more I am at peace with all those around me. When I am in touch with the beautiful energy of my higher self, I see the whole world through the eyes of beauty and feel good. When I am not following my truth and am some way feeling frustrated, I tend to see the world that way.

I am so proud of you dear one. Remember how I would get upset with you when I felt you weren't living all the truth you knew. Now I can see how you are and how much you want to. You're so grateful for the guidance you receive to move through your life. It is very beautiful to watch how you find your way out so quickly. You have set yourself up well to be in those situations. I know it may seem like things are moving too slow for you, but all the timing is on purpose. Just always continue to reach for your soul self and keep forging that relationship. That is what it is like. You're attracting the soul parts like one would collect bricks to build a house and then you hold it together with cement until it is dried and solidly connected. Or like a bird collects sticks for its nest. You're collecting your selves.

Dealing with Anger

June 12

Hello, beloved,

I have felt you with me today during my challenge: I felt you guiding me (after an argument with a friend). I am glad you're with me. Forgive me if at times I still miss your physical presence, the arms that would comfort me, the soft lips that would kiss me.

Even with you, I didn't understand totally how to deal with the energy of anger. It's an emotional energy that needs to be expressed if felt; all emotions are to be honored, I know it's okay to have anger. If it's okay to have it, then it's okay to express it. So then it comes to what is the best way to express it. Uncontrollable anger can be very destructive but sometimes destruction can be beneficial, even if it may not seem that way at the time. I know I don't like the energy of anger when I am around it. It's not very pleasurable to me.

Quite often when I try to understand anger I think of the story of Jesus and the moneychangers *(Matthew 21:12)*. It was the only part in the Bible that I remember Jesus getting angry. The story tells of Jesus overthrowing tables and yelling at the coin changers that they have turned his fathers' holy temple into a market place. I had always figured if Jesus got angry it must be okay. After all, if he went around to all the men and politely asked them to leave they would have laughed in his face.

Do we just have our anger, witness the way it has been expressed, and if the results are favorable, then use it as the tool that is needed? If we do, and it causes a deep pain, do we just have compassion and hope they understand?

And what about how I feel about getting angry? Or what have I learned from being at the receiving end of anger? Certain times when I have received anger, I have either gotten angry back as a defense, or broken down emotionally. It seems very close to a physical attack. Then I seem to question if it's okay to physically attack; are wars okay?

Even war, people say has its value. If we don't ever really die and all that happens is that people choose to go to another dimension, then why would it be judged as being so bad?

Then it comes to the question, "is this anger an energy I want to experience more or less of, like the sadness of your death?" I experienced a lot of sadness, into its very depths, and it was very deep and profound and there was a value in the experience- to remember compassion for people when they are troubled, and to realize we don't ever know how that may look.

I've experienced anger at its depths. The value, I suppose, as I feel with the situation is it gives me a sense of power at a time when I feel I need it. My preference though, now that I think about it, is not to add anymore negative energy to the world. I would rather add the energy of love to the world and promote world peace beginning with my own energy.

I remember hearing one of my yoga teacher's, Swami Satchidanada say that anger was a tool to be kept in one's pocket and to use only when needed. And that we could use it, giving the effect of being angry without actually letting the anger affect us. I think that would be a good goal, to be able to use it if one needs to give off a sense of power, like in the example of disciplining children.

Robert Monroe, in his book, *The Ultimate Journey*, says the key to emotions are to experience all of them and subsequently learn to control and direct them as desired. This seems to be the answer. I don't want to feel the energy of anger in my system so the answer would be to be able to control it and still be able to use it if I need to feel a sense of strength in a particular situation. Also remembering I know that peace in the world does begin with each one of us, and if I do expect there to be peace in the world, I certainly have to find a way to achieve if first within my own being.

Menstrual Cycle

June 13

Hello my Bear,

Well, things are much lighter and freer today. Thank you for all of your assistance the last few days, some of what has been written and some of which has not. So back to the time of your journey into the spirit world.

I also remember that when I was by myself I could sense you around more, only I didn't get much time alone. I had four protective, nurturing caring woman watching over me carefully. The only time I was alone was on trips to the post office or store. It was then I would have conversations with you in the car. We would talk about you leaving. We would discuss things just like when you were physically here. Like

77

when we used to joke with each other about who was the meanest. I told you that you were definitely the meanest for going off and dying. The conversation would switch from joking to arguing to sadness to crying. I could feel how it saddened you when I cried.

One thing that made me curious, and also doubt myself, was why I didn't feel your energy as strongly as I thought I would. I'm usually very good at feeling energy. I could sense you in a subtle way but not as energetically as I had hoped. I would share with those around me some of my experiences with you and the guidance and insight, but I could also feel their doubts. Their skepticism is understandable; it's not as if talking to a dead person is an everyday occurrence. Now that I look back, there is less doubt on what I felt. Maybe some of it had to do with me being in a weakened state, and perhaps you too had not built up your spiritual body. Recently, I have had energy experiences with you that there was no room for doubt because it was so strong.

I remember, I kept asking you to make some kind of phenomenon happen. I have heard stories of people who have seen visions of their loved ones appear to them. I had hoped maybe you could make something move or appear. I sensed from you that it was not an easy thing for you to do. There may be others who have the skill to do that, but it was one you would have to develop.

Such a quiet day, it's the first day of my menstrual cycle. Even you finally learned it was best for me to be quiet. It took me a long time to learn and now it seems so clear. When a woman has her blood flow, her energy moves inward, quiet and reflective. It is a time best kept to herself, unless she is with another who understands the gentleness of the space. It is a time for a woman to reach in and nurture herself, or connect with the nurturing spirit of the Mother Earth. How much would be made easier if we all understood this cycle?

I remember how after our time of adjusting to being in a relationship with each other, we still ended up getting into an argument around my period. This was because it is a time I didn't feel as nurturing as I usually was, but a time for me to be nurtured. It seems to take so much for a man to become the nurturer. It seems best for a man to understand this woman's space as much as possible. I'm sure many men have experienced the fire of the woman when they try to pull on her as she is moving into this space. Of course it is also a large lesson for me to understand that I must also respect this space for myself.

While Trance Dancing in Switzerland, I received a clear message for me to move into this understanding of the mysteries of the menstrual cycle. I have heard that in the old days it was considered a time of a woman's power and to be respected. Women would gather together in what they called a moon hut. They would receive visions or messages to guide the community; and the wisdom would be honored.

I know that, at times, on the first day of my flow I am extremely receptive to the energy around me, all of the sounds, I feel inside me. If there are inharmonious sounds around me, I feel them and it rattles my space. I know our society is not set up for this type of honoring. I was lucky enough that after a while I always happened to have that day off and I would stay home by myself and be so grateful I could have quiet space. The problem arose when you came home and I wasn't giving you the energy and attention you were used to from me. I didn't feel like greeting you at the door or even to cook dinner. I was torn between my feelings of wanting to be with you and with myself. But to be with you, only if you could nurture me instead of me nurturing you. Those times when I did try to do what I normally did for you it didn't usually work out. I wasn't clear enough in my own needs at that time to be able to communicate them to you so there would be less misunderstandings around that time. Even now I catch myself with the same patterns of taking care of others and not minding my space.

I can understand why you would be confused when you normally see your woman nurturing and caring, and one day she says today I don't feel that way. I can see where you could feel hurt and take it personally. The mystery of the woman's menstrual cycle and the cycles of the moon as it takes the tides in and out must be more understood. There is a lot missing in the world as a result of it. I know there is a lot more I will still learn, and what I have learned so far has helped me to understand myself, life, relationships, cycles, women, and more.

Here honor appears again. Honoring myself and my menstrual cycle, and the thirty-day moon cycle it is some-how connected with. How much are we missing by being so caught up in daily activities that we do not take the time to feel and hear the selves (connected to cells) that are within us? Do sometimes we purposely close ourselves off because we do not want to hear what the voice is saying? Do we resist doing what it calls upon us to do for the caring of our soul?

It still amazes me when women who spend a lot of time together end up having their menstrual cycles at the same time. That used to happen when I lived with my sisters. The other thing is when women get their period at the same time as the full moon or the new moon. I have had my cycles with both. Again, I heard in the old days when women spent more time outdoors with nature their cycles would be in alignment with the moon. Birth control would be so much easier because a woman's fertile time would be in tune with the moon cycle.

I find it fascinating to be around women who are about to get their period and get into a cleaning mode. It happens so much and quite often unconsciously. My sister and I always joke with each other about what we end up cleaning right before our cycles begin. Sometimes we end up cleaning out closets, or getting at corners that hardly get thought of, and almost always end up having a desire to clean the bathtub. I think if women paid attention to this they would realize how they are preparing their space.

And so, now, beloved one, whose voice has been silent as

I have been searching my life. Tell me, dear one, who has a vision now that is beyond the one that I live in. Do I want to try to be patient? How can I make decisions when things are changing so rapidly? How can I decide when the truth is not known because it changes and transforms like the weather? Sunny and hot one day and cold and rainy another. How do I know what is best for me, and what is needed for me to move through and learn? When we were going through our troubled times, I knew for sure what I would not accept and we fought a war until I retreated into myself and my soul was my only comfort. I seemed to struggle to have to keep it around me. Is it like that now? Another dark night of my soul, given to me to reach for and pull over me as a blanket in the cold of winter? Are you there now as part of that blanket, rather than the one who has been used by the universe to move me there? It is very comforting to have you there to always pull near me, rather than the one whom I've had to separate from to move towards my soul. But hasn't it been enough already, this darkness? Isn't it time for me to be out in the light feeling the warmth of the sun? Is there still more I must do? Spring is here. I have made it through winter. Summer is shortly upon me. When do I get to go out and swim in the joy now that the winter coldness is behind me? Or is it still like the weather here high in the mountain forests, partly sunny, but often cloudy? Warmer outside than it is inside. There is such a restlessness moving me inward because outward the road seems blocked. It is causing me to look within my own soul to see what it is I want to bring out with me. I know what I want. I want joy. I want creativity and to create. I want the peace of feeling the connection to my soul at all times. I want to feel the abundance of life.

I don't try to picture how it should look as much as we used to. I keep seeing, more and more, how it seems more purposeful to look for the feelings I want to have in my life and send those messages out to the universe. Still co-creating with the universe, I do want to experience love in my heart overflowing out into the world. I don't know what a relationship should look like anymore. I knew what I wanted ours to look like because we both mostly wanted the same thing. To us, our love was the most important but it took us a while to get to that point.

I remember right before our marriage ceremony I was in a space of struggling with finances because of the extra expense of the wedding. There were things I wanted, and I wasn't sure I should spend the money. You caught me in that space of not feeling happy in the moment and asked for confirmation from me that the most important thing in our life was our love. Your question surprised me and put me back into perspective and back into my heart, so I could look you in the eyes and honestly say that our love was the most important thing to be honored at this time in life. What good does it do to go into a negative space about financial concerns?

Do I want that again? I know I cannot have exactly what we had because you were uniquely you. You knew how important it was to have me in your life.

You had begun to accompany me out into the world, working with the people with healings, firewalks, sweat lodges and classes. We were moving together with you being my healing partner beside me. You always honored my wisdom and felt proud to have me by your side. And I was proud of you to be a man who could honor the wisdom of the feminine and intuition and not have your ego interfere.

So what is it that I want? Is it to take time to be by myself again the way I did before we got together. I swore I didn't want the pain of relationships again after the pain of separation of a loved one long ago. You were my first real relationship after that hurt. But I had done much work to move through that pain to heal and free myself again.

As you know I have been given the gift of a relationship with an old friend and there have been many misunderstandings. Is this just a temporary gift ? Do I move on without it or take it along with me? Do I even have that decision? Will the universe decide for itself? Perhaps if I just keep praying for my soul to keep its blanket around me, praying for joy, love, peace, and abundance, then I'll just move into that and have my answer. Perhaps that is my answer. When the world seems to turn in on me, I go in and seek the joy, like the seed that is planted underground seeks the light. I feel it is a true calling of my soul, the call for joy.

As I write these words, I call out to my soul for the joy to come in and circle me and fill my heart and my cells and my life, to bring laughter and fun, singing and dancing, to balance the pain and sorrow and crying. It has had its value and now it is time for something else. This is what I call out to you my soul, my light, my life, bring me joy. Allow me to experience the joy of living. Allow me to experience the gift that you have left for me, the urge to find the lightness of life. Even as I find joy I can also share that with the one that has left me, to find it on my own, from my own source. In this way it cannot be taken away or threatened and truly be shared.

My beloved Loryn,

I clap my hands and rejoice as you come to these realizations. Remember that spirit has carried you and taken care of you when I left the physical world. Trust it as it continues to carry you. Ask and it will carry you on its wings, as a beautiful butterfly exploring the magnificence of nature.

You are not left alone. There are many spirits around you supporting you. They urge you up into the light and the freedom that joy brings to the soul. I have watched you and at times have remained silent, allowing you the space to explore your own self.

Decisions are not meant to be made now, as you have sensed. Use the energy of your circumstances now to pull you out of the shadows and into the light. Your time of darkness is almost over. Use it wisely to create

I ask now the voice of the pain what it has to say to me. It says that it is the pain of not feeling the freedom of my heart; like it has been shut off and clamped down. Like the voice of the mountain looking down on me, telling me I cannot walk the earth beneath its feet... giving my love out where it is not honored.

This pattern I have seen before in past relationships, where there didn't seem to be a balance of giving and receiving. A part of it, I believe, was me being better at giving than receiving. For me it took a lot of surrendering in order to be able to receive. Some of us have to learn how to give more, some to give more freely, and some to be able to receive more graciously. All of our lessons are different.

With us, I was grateful for a love that we learned to honor, a love that allowed you to fulfill your destiny of experiencing love on this planet, and move me to fulfill mine. How grateful I am to be a part of that love.

So now, my Bear, I will go and dance and pray and call once again the joy to fill me as I dance with my soul. Will you come and join me in the dance? Will you call the joy with me?

Yes, as you know. Thank you, beloved, for being with me. I am glad we are in communication.

(Afterthoughts)

How many times does one forgive? How long will one allow abuse before one has to say it is enough? How many times does one believe when another promises to change and never do it again, only for it to happen again the next day? How do we know what will change and what won't? It is said one should never expect someone else to change, yet how far does the acceptance go before we are not honoring ourselves? It seems the only answer is to pray for a better life, go day by day, and keep our ears open for that inner voice that guides and can be trusted. That voice that says, "okay, enough is enough."

Love is Healing

June 17

Hello beloved,

It's so nice to have you around me and to have you pop up here and there and quite often make me laugh.

One thing that had been really healing for me in our relationship was your acceptance of the many ways I had been judged before, either by myself or others. One was my emotional self. You loved that part of me that was sensitive and cried, a part of me that I had perceived as being weak. Your acceptance was such a relief and such a healing.

Then my tendency towards being possessive. Growing up with two brothers and two sisters, I had seemed to always be trying to protect my things from being taken, and

sometimes broken or ruined. I've always seemed to be trying to protect my space from people who take without asking. As I grow spiritually, I've realized I am trying to get
more of a sense of my own space and keep it sacred and
respected. But that has to be done myself first; then the
world is more apt to reflect it.

You also accepted my possessiveness of you. In fact, you
loved it, taking it as a compliment. I remember you telling
me how you bragged to your friends how this beautiful
woman wanted you all to herself. Your acceptance of this,
dear one, was also very healing.

All of a sudden, all the teachings of how this was to be
judged as wrong, could now be seen in a way it would be
accepted and healed. I've realized so many teachings I've
learned have only been partially true.

I also accepted your jealousy and never made you feel
wrong for it, but understood it and worked with it. We both
created a sacred space within our relationship because of
these feelings. It took us a while to find where the limita-
tions or boundaries of these feelings could go.

Some of your friends had a difficult time with this, but
after you died most of them understood. That space we cre-

ated was what we needed to have, not knowing consciously, that we would only have a short time together. I felt how we were doing things was right and I held my strength against the judgments. After your death, all judgments were dropped, all was understood, and more healing of relationships took place.

More and more, I see how we cannot judge appropriately another situation because what may be okay for one may not be the best for another. Each person has such a unique path to walk. And we can only see that path if we have the ability to step into a higher level of vision where there is no right or wrong. Everything just is, where the world of duality falls away into the world of unity.

I pray and pray that I may have my vision live in this place above duality where there is no judgment: just love, acceptance and understanding. I know there are still complications from that space but at least it's closer to the truth, and it's more heart-centered rather than mind-centered.

Fate vs. Free-Will

June 19

Hello, my beloved,

Going back once again to the time of your death, you died on a Friday. Your death was considered suspicious so they had to do an autopsy which couldn't be done until Monday. We then tried to see if they could do it first on Monday (there were two others to be done). We were trying to get the services done because your mom had a plane ticket to go back on Wednesday. It ended up that she changed her flight arrangements to stay a few days longer. What I kept thinking in the back of my mind was how often I heard about how different cultures wait three days before they do anything to the body. Some say it's to give the spirit time to fully leave the body. I don't know how much validity that has but I felt it may have all been in divine order for us to have to wait before the body was cremated.

The other thing that happened which created a lot of turmoil was your mom's phone call to the doctor, the one you and I had gone to a week before your death because of your chest pains. The words he said to you still continue to run through my mind, "You have nothing to worry about; you're in your prime; you're strong and healthy." He must have said that to you about three times while we were there. He said, "just take this antibiotic medication, and if you still have the pains in two weeks, come back and we will run tests." Well, obviously two weeks was too late.

I remember you still complaining of your chest pains. You had stopped smoking because you thought maybe that was the problem. We decided we just had to wait another week because that was what the doctor said. How foolish, I can see, it can be to place our lives in another's hand, just because he has the name doctor. And how much responsibility the doctors have. One mistake can take a person's life.

Your mom, having a lot of experience working with the

medical profession, called your doctor with the pain of your death in her heart. She wanted to understand why he chose not to take tests. You went in and complained of chest pains (and a cough) and had a history of heart attacks in the family. Plus, you were overweight, and had not lived a healthy lifestyle for many years, including smoking since a teenager. Also your dad had his first heart attack at age thirty-eight and had died a few years back. She wanted to understand why he didn't choose to do something that might have saved your life. His response to her was that he promised her that her son never complained of chest pains. He denied it!

Well, that caused both me and your mom to get upset because he was obviously lying. But I guess what can you expect him to say, "Well, yes, he did, and I'm sorry; I just didn't think he would have a heart problem at age thirty-three so I didn't test him. I'm sorry my decision might have cost your son's life." It would take quite a man to be able to admit that.

I met a young man and his family at my moving sale. They said they had the same doctor as you. The young man went into the clinic for pain in his intestines. The doctor wanted to give him some pain medication (he was on call at the time), and have him come back. After this doctor left the room the other doctors and nurses told the young man not to do it. If he took pain medication and had an appendicitis attack it would not be good. So the family went back and had to argue with the doctor to do something now. The doctor looked at his watch and mumbled something about how he wouldn't have time to do the paperwork he had to do, but finally complied.

If this is the same doctor as they said, he seems to have a pattern of putting things off, take this medication now and come back later. These are serious misjudgments for people to make. We place our lives in their hands. When someone dies there are many gifts or things to learn as a result of their death. I can only hope that your death has awakened this doctor into becoming much more careful in his decision-making.

It brings up questions, is absolutely every little thing part of the divine plan? How can there be free will and destiny simultaneously? Was your death pure fate or did you have a choice? Ultimately there is a higher power and we also have free will.

These questions have been present for many years. I remember reading an article years ago explaining how there are certain parts of our life that are destiny. It was locked in by a code and these codes opened at certain points in our life. Certain pathways were open for choice and certain memories would awaken at different times in our life.

For example, perhaps it was my destiny or fate that at the age of thirty-five I would go to the Big Island of Hawaii. It seemed so, since I was literally brought there. Perhaps much of the first five months was free will; then it was again destiny that June 28, 1993 we would meet at a party. It cost $50 to attend which I really couldn't afford. Nonetheless, I ended up being invited to go for free. You also had your own story of how you ended up there.

I will always remember that night we met. We had eye contact the moment I walked in the door. My girlfriend kept telling me that you were watching me from the corner of the room. Finally, you asked me to dance and three hours later you asked me to marry you. Of course, it was pretty funny the next day when you had to admit you forgot my name, but it was understandable because I told you my spiritual name, Solana, and many people have a difficult time

with that. So I said you could call me by my family name,
Loryn if it were easier for you.

For the next two years and three weeks we were together
every day except for ten days, seven of which was when I
went to my sister's wedding. We knew from the very beginning we were meant to be together. We were both scared
because everything moved so fast. There was a knowingness
of a love that needed time to catch up with it.

I had a reading with a Vedic astrologer to see if the reading could help shed some light on my lessons around your
death. He said it was possible that we had set it up that you
would die soon after marriage; if we had held off on marriage you might have lived longer. These seemed like very
insensitive things to say to a woman still grieving the loss
of her husband. I understood how firmly he believed in his
astrology as being infallible. I didn't feel like getting into a
philosophical discussion at the time, or challenging his beliefs. Doesn't astrology also follow destiny and free will?
Where you're destined to have a certain experience in a
particular time period in your life, but it could turn up in a
hundred different ways? The way it turns out will be determined by the level of awareness you use to handle the situ-

ation.

Is it worth the effort to contemplate the total meaning of your death? Either way, it is something I must accept; knowing the grace of God still runs through my life. A friend of mine from Singapore told me once that it is not <u>why</u> things happen to us but <u>how we handle them</u> that is important. Those words have hung true often through my life. Perhaps it is not necessary for us to have all the whys answered. Perhaps it would benefit us to allow some of the mysteries to remain. Instead, we can focus on handling the situation the best we can. When we look for the value and see them as gifts, then perhaps the whys will get answered.

Sacred Sexuality

June 21

So, dear one,

What shall we discuss today? The art of lovemaking? Our love for each other moved us through a lot of our sexual issues. You were very open from the start to my viewpoint on sexuality being sacred and ways to spiritualize the act. I was very relieved at this. Still, I had to work through many trust issues.

Breathing the energy up through our spine to prolong lovemaking became a habit for us. We would stop when the energy became very powerful and take deep breaths and visualize the energy moving from the base of our spine into our hearts and then imagine that heart energy flowing into each other. We would feel and see the love in each others eyes. Oh dear one, it makes my heart overflow just writing about it. How many sexual love relationships would improve if just this one pattern was established?

After lovemaking you stayed with me and cuddled in the afterglow, the cocoon of energy that surrounded us afterward. You understood not to get up abruptly as I was very aware of the energy meld. It was like the sharpness of tearing off a Band-Aid, if you moved away too quickly or too soon. I've heard it said that many men turn over or fall asleep or get up and smoke a cigarette afterwards. That, perhaps, is an avoidance of feeling the deeper intimacy of the sacred sharing. But after you understood, you stayed with me and seemed also to delight in the energy as much as I.

You always made love looking into my eyes, relishing not only the feelings within your body but also the one you were sharing yourself with. You were such a gentle lover to me and I began to open more and more of what I had kept closed for years.

It was very difficult for me when my energy got so out of balance because of other challenges in my life, that my thyroid pretty much quit working. My sexual energy, normally at that time being low, became almost nil. Your feelings of being loved and having sex I knew were so closely connected. You always felt so much more loved after we made love, and showed it in your affections. This connection was so strong that when we didn't make love as often, you had to deal with your feelings. You had to realize that I still loved you, even if we didn't make love.

I had to deal with my feelings of worthiness as a woman and my sexuality. I knew at times you felt hurt, and I felt hurt because you didn't seem to be able to understand. I wanted to give you what you wanted but my body didn't want to respond.

In time, after the help of medication, my energy started to awaken again. And strangely enough one of our most beautiful experiences was the magical three hours of lovemaking just a few days before your death.

Being with you really motivated me to want to be more open sexually. I know I really was able to open up with you more than I had ever had before. I felt I could trust you. I could also feel how important it was for you in the sense of feeling a closer connection in our relationship. For you it was much more than just a physical need. I wanted lovemaking to be a sacred act, which went along with what my inner self had been telling me all my sexual life, but my culture didn't support. I realize everyone doesn't have that feeling, but I do. And I was much more committed to living my truth rather than going along with what my heart wasn't into. We worked through many sexual issues. And it put you more in your truth to see where you were in your sexual self. After we were both more clear and more in our own power on where we were sexually, we were able to move into deeper and deeper levels. We both were such powerful influences in healing parts of our own sexual nature. We finally got to a point where I saw you as really clear in wanting to make love for the experience of feeling that deep level of love that nurtured you. I was then willing to open to deeper levels of my own sexuality to have greater experiences with you. It didn't happen as great as I would have loved it to, but I could see where it was such a big step for me. I at least had a great desire to open up and that is the first step to calling it in as a form of prayer.

Although our sexual relationship was good, my sexual energy wasn't as high as yours. I do realize that my energy brought yours more into a balanced state where you gained a tremendous amount of self control, which you loved seeing and experiencing for yourself. Realizing that your sexual energy no longer had control over you, you had learned to master your own energy. You did so well. I was always much more attracted to men who were in control of their energy. So much hardship has been caused in this world because people haven't been trained and educated in handling their sexual energy. I had so much respect for the work you did on yourself, and it all allowed me to trust you so much more. I had always been sensitive to the difference in the energy of when a man was coming on to me with a desire to share love or a desire just to have sex. The energy is just so different. There isn't necessarily anything wrong with that if both partners agree. With my particular issues, I needed a man to come to me with a heart energy. This energy created a trust that allowed my sexual energy to open. Through my Tantra studies, I realized I needed to teach you this instead of me just expecting you to know. You were very open to learning, because you wanted deep, sexual, loving experiences as much as I did. I was so grateful that your ego didn't block your way to being open to learning new levels of sexual/

spiritual experiences.

I loved when we did the nurturing meditation and could feel how it would harmonize our energies. We would lie on our sides and you would snuggle up behind me. You would call in the light and ask to be used as a channel of healing and then use your imagination and intention to breathe the light into the crown chakra at the top of your head into your heart. Then you would breathe the light from your heart into mine as you exhaled and I would simultaneously be exhaling and using my intention to bring your love into the depth of my heart, hold it a few seconds and then as I inhaled I would sent it into the depths of your heart. Oh it felt so intimate to breathe into each other's hearts. I could feel such a deep pure love coming into me and I would send the love of my heart that was combined with the Divine love of God as I sent it with the light. Sometimes we would combine it with the prayers, "I open myself to fully receive your love and I fully give my love to you." Then we would do the same thing at all the other chakras. I could feel how our energies would balance each other's. Then we would switch the breath to alternating breathing, where I was inhaling as you were exhaling, imagining our spines full of light and breathing that light fully into each other. It was amazing how close I would feel to you. It was as if our energies were one and there was not a physical body separating us. Then the last part we would face each other and just share love with our eyes. It felt so pure, so sacred, and so powerful.

Sometimes we would just lay face-to-face and just breathe light into each other's hearts. I really loved doing that also. It was always so comforting to feel such pure loving coming from each other's hearts. Thank you again Bear for all the love you shared with me and for all the times you loved me with such pure divine love. I am truly grateful for all the moments of deep love we shared.

Higher Selves

June 22

Hello, my beloved,

Once again I am comforted by your presence. At this time last year we were doing the firewalk in honor of our wedding ceremony and preparing for the sweat lodge ceremony, also in honor of our wedding. These activities seem a much better way to honor marriage then the traditional bachelor party. I remember the comments from people on how they could see and feel the love that we had. People could look at us as a couple and feel the love radiating from us. We were honored to be each others partner and it showed. How grateful I am to have had the experience of love that we had. And I know we worked on it to be that way. There had been a few big challenges that we had to overcome or move through, but we both had the strong desire to experience love and unity, and we wanted to do it with each other. And almost every day we reminded each other and ourselves that we were grateful to God for the light of love that was brought through each other. Our connection to God was our strength and our comfort.

One of the things that amazed me about you was how fast you picked up on things. When we met, I had over fifteen years of different metaphysical, mind development and spiritual healing training. Things that took years for me to grow confidence in, you picked up quickly. For example, our meditative form of traveling out of body to other dimensions. Shamanism calls it journeying. You were willing to try it. We laid down next to each other holding hands, eyes closed, taking many slow deep breaths to help shift our consciousness, feelings our spirits freer and freer, imagining ourselves moving up into a column of light, continuing to go higher and higher. We would always ask our spiritual guides and the angels to come and assist us into the higher realms of light and love. Then we would place our intention to ask for where or what we wanted in the meditation. Many times I would ask to move to be with the Pleiadians because I had connected with them so many times previously. I was very familiar with them and they loved to be of assistance to help humanity. I was a little nervous because I knew many things I was sharing with you in my life at first seems quite odd, so I was not sure how you would react. What amazed me was you ended up to be a natural and had memories of traveling as a child and visiting the Pleiadians as we had done. You even discovered a way for us to move through one level and go even higher. If higher is the best term to be used.

When I first met the Pleiadians it was while I was taking a group of people in meditation. They all seemed to have a Pleiadian connection. Some people believe they are actually our ancestors. I heard of a Native American tribe that taught their anesctors came from the stars, namely the Pleiadians. I certainly had my doubts when we first contacted them. I could feel their sincerity and their desire to help and they also helped many of us heal and balance the energies in our bodies during the meditation. It was just I was not willing to turn my total trust over to these ETs right away. It took me a while to get used to the idea. In the group meditations I would call in the Pleiadians and people would get all sorts of information, even about their space ships. I had maintained a manner of non-attached observation, until one day after about 3 months of regular contact they finally got to me during our group meditation. I saw these two human looking, attractive, adult Pleiadians with blond hair. They showed me this beautiful young blond girl, and for some reason seeing her brought back a memory of a deep love. Somehow, I felt she was my sister and it brought tears to my eyes. Now I had no idea how this was possible but it felt so true in my heart. The only answer I could come up with was somehow we could live in alternate realities and I had some other life simultaneously connected with the Pleiadeans. Of course I have no way to verify this but after that experience it made me more open and loving towards them. So when you told me you remember them from your childhood I was amazed.

I loved when we visited the cloud beings. The memories still stay strongly with me. Once again we separated our consciousness from our body or earth plane existence and asked to be led to a place that would most benefit us at that time. We ended up in a world of white fluffy clouds, like one would see out of an airplane window. A man who reminded me of Merlin the Magician lovingly met us. He had a gray beard, wore a long blue robe and a wizard hat. He took us up to the top of a narrow steep stairway in a castle-like tower. Honey, as I review our trip it certainly sounds strange but when we were there it felt so real. There was no doubting the experience. We looked out the window and saw an overview of the vast land of the cloud community. He communicated to us through what seemed like mental telepathy connected with feelings. Their level of consciousness was much higher than I would have expected. They were a group of beings that had a body so unlike ours. We learned acceptance and patience from them. Their way of life was mostly very slow with great awareness and compassion. It seemed as they past over our lands they had this great understanding of a more expansive way of life. We gained a lot of respect for them as conscious beings. I didn't understand why we went there until later when we moved up into the mountains. Up there the clouds surrounded our house every afternoon. I seem to understand the American Indian tradition of communing with all parts of nature much more from that experience.

The other thing I loved was when we went up together and communed with what we called our higher selves. Again we would travel up into the light and ask to meet and to communicate with the highest aspect of ourselves. Up we would go higher and higher, feeling freer and freer, our spirits leaving our bodies behind. We traveled into realms of greater light and greater love. My higher self appeared as this absolutely beautiful, shining, loving light being. I could sense such love and acceptance from her through this warm light energy that flowed into me. She was so wise and patient and understanding. She would tell me things like how I needed to accept myself more and see my own inner beauty. I know she is a reflection of me and sometimes I would cry seeing the depth of beauty she had. If we had some problem we needed assistance on, especially on our relationship, we could go and ask our higher selves for insight. Amazingly, almost every time, your higher self gave you insights on things about yourself, about me, and about our relationship that you had never thought of, or realized in normal consciousness. And it always helped us out tremendously. I was used to being able to get answers, but to be able to do it with you and have such immediate results was wonderful.

One thing that you did show was a great desire for us to make our relationship work. It really does take two people together to want to work through things. Having such an effective tool helped. It also allowed us a way to put our own hurt feelings aside and turn it over to a higher energy. We just both had to be willing to do that. Having a spiritual partnership with you then and now is, and was, a true blessing. I am grateful. Thank you, God.

My dear Beloved, Loryn,

Thank you for honoring me as you have. You truly were a blessing my last years on earth. You woke me up out of a deep sleep, stirring within me the memories of who I was. Your guidance and love and caring nurtured me back to my true Self that had felt wounded for many years. Your love healed my wounds and gave me strength to live again. Even if I didn't live much longer on earth, my spirit was awakened. In your challenging times I also would see through your pain and bring you back in your times of memory lapses of your true Self.

I am grateful for such a beautiful love in my life.

Yes, at times I know I was quite selfish and that hurt you, but your love just softened me again. I respect and honor you for the part you played in my life the short time we had together physically. Your endless love could move me into states of ecstasy for finally finding the love I was searching for.

As I watch you, I pray for the best for you. I ask this love to continue to flow into your life, that you move more and more into the ecstasy of the divinity and sacredness of love. I pray that you also may wholly awaken to your true Self and see that your life can really be filled with the love, peace, health, joy and abundance you desire and deserve.

I love when you reconnect with the ecstasy of our love in your meditations, the love that is the connection of the universe. I am grateful that our love can bring you to that place. May that energy move more fully into your life so that your life may be truly happy. And, my dear one, I serenely await your arrival here with me, when you have finished your joyful task on the planet.

My love has been and always will be with you.

Thank you, Rock, for being with me.

Uniqueness

June 23 , 1996

Hello, beloved,

Even though I speak (write) to you each day it seems like such a long time. I do wonder what it's like for you to live in an existence without time. I was blessed to have a friend like you to live with on this earth. I do miss your friendship. It's such a different life when one has someone that is their companion, one that enjoys the other's company the most.

Not that we each didn't have our own interests. You would work in your workshop, creating, while I would be busy around the house, doing things like yoga, painting, creating in our room of sacred space, dancing, reading, cooking or beautifying (cleaning) our home. Occasionally, you would go out and play golf. But most of all, besides working, we were usually together and happy to be so. I used to love it when we would sit outside on our porch and watch those magnificent gold and pink colored Hawaiian sunsets over the ocean.

When we moved into the house in the clouds, just three months before your death, we had a whole new range of activities we did together; feeding and taking care of the horses; especially the pregnant one. We would sit outside and watch all the cows in the huge, beautiful green field behind our house. We created and cared for a vegetable and herb garden. It was very sad for me to look at the garden after your death. It just didn't seem as exciting, since you were not there with me to enjoy it. Our favorite was making and watching a fire in our fireplace. I loved smelling the rosemary we would burn in it from our huge rosemary bush outside.

There definitely are many challenges involved in relationships. I've heard it said that is a quick way to grow spiritually and I agree, only if one does it with awareness to learn about ourselves. There are so many of our own issues thrown up into our face to look at, and then there is a deep love that heals the wounds.

After your death, I thought that I would never be able to have a relationship like ours again. And that's probably true, because you and I were a unique combination. So every relationship is unique. As I told you many times when you were here, you were a wonderful man, both sensitive and also very strong. And now like your name Rock, you're a strength to me.

Thank you beloved for loving me and being there for me, both when you were here and while you are there.

Shifting the Energy

June 24

Hello, dear one,

Thank you for being present when there doesn't seem to be anything else at hand. Sometimes it seems all that was once here is lost, like there is nothing to hold onto. Perhaps it is time to find the thing that is always present - the energy of my soul, the love, the ecstasy, the joy. I know it is always here when I choose to focus on it. It's always at hand when I dance. It's all always present. It's a matter of focusing on it, desiring it more and bringing it into my life.

Sometimes it seems that these are the times it is most important to shift the energy, to call in the new energy.

Hello, my honeybee,

My sweet, sweet honey. Like nectar to a bee. Your beauty is like the flower to the bee.

You shine a light that attracts to you those that love the energy that you give. Your nature is to love, give, and care. I was always amazed at your capacity to love.

Your heart is so very delicate and gentle. You must keep it handled with the tenderest care. My love, your sweetness is sweeter then the sweetest honey.

Tap into the beauty of your being. There you will know your rightful place. Struggling is not necessary, only soulful joining and recognition of all that you are. Bring it forward. I support you in this, beloved.

Our purposes were different for our life but, the importance that we played in each others lives are the same. You assisted me in moving me forward in my awakening of love in my life in a very short period. I was able to accomplish what I came to earth to do: to know love. You naturally have a heart that knows love. After a while I was able to see that part of you even through your troubled times. Remember how I used to say something when you were sad or angry, "Where's my Bee? What did you do with her? I know she's in there. Where is that loving woman I know so well?" And that would usually bring you back out, because it is your nature. So for me, you were an example of love and a partner to share in this love. We did share lots of love that helped us move through the troubled times.

And now for you, your purpose is to know joy. My assistance to you, dear one, is to help guide you from here. My part has been in the feeling of loss and deep sadness that hopefully will catapult you into that same depth of joyousness. You have many reasons to be joyous about life. We still have our love which is incredibly joyful. You have gained incredible strength moving through your trials. You have energy, health, love and abundance. You have beauty and caring. You feel more connected to mother nature and your spirit/soul, which is in actuality all the same thing.

It's all about reconnecting with all parts of yourself and moving forward. It's like now your car is fixed. Yet there were many things checked and changed and much time was spent examining it. And just like the simplicity of changing a thought that is outworn to one that

*works better, simply changing a worn out part in your
car makes it work again. It was just a matter of finding out which part needed to be changed.*

(reunion-Monroe Institute)

Thank you, beloved, for your words of encouragement.
When you tell me of your love and appreciation for me, it
just brings tears to my eyes to feel so loved. It seems to help
heal the hurt and pain and harshness that believing in the
illusion of the earth plane can bring.

I used to think that as one became an enlightened being
that it meant one had no pains, but only joy, like, living in a
continuous joyous state of being. Now, I'm not so sure that
is the case. Perhaps, as humans, we are meant to experience all ranges of emotions and even to delight in all the
possible ranges of experiences. We also learn to live more
and more in a joyous state. It is like having more awareness with the witness experiencing pain and at the same
time knowing its not all real. Then perhaps that
knowingness is what leads us out of staying there so long.

At first, after your death, I had lapses of extreme sadness with times of numbness. The first month I chose to sell

everything and I had to deal with placing many ads, interviewing people for your business, garage sales, and other mundane things. During this time, it was as if I was being held by some energy that was guiding me and carrying me through it all. Having so many things to take care of and keep me busy, I know was a blessing. I had only a month to sell all the furniture, all the many tools, the boat, the cars, and your business. Brenda (my sister) had only a month before she had to return to school in New Jersey and I knew it was best for me not to be alone.

The second month I spent in Florida with Mari and her husband. I kept busy by helping them out with their business, mostly assisting my sister in using the computer.

In October, I visited my girlfriend Grace, her husband and their new son, Maxwell. I went to watch her store for her while her employee went on vacation. For the first time I was not kept busy. It was a slow time in the store and it just seemed like an avalanche hit me. I had thought perhaps it was all over, the grieving, because I seemed okay. Then I realized it was because I had stayed busy. Now with hours and hours of alone time I moved into an extremely sensitive state. I cried at the drop of a hat. I felt incapable of handling stress.

One day a man came in who told me he had lost his wife. I could relate to many of his experiences as he spoke to me about the difficulties he dealt with around his wifes' death. On the way out he said something that rang true deep inside me. He said, "make sure you keep talking about it." I knew he was right. It seemed the more I spoke of it the lighter it became.

Then the next month, I finally had something to be excited about. I was going to the Monroe Institute. It was one of the places you and I dreamed of going. One day, while still in Hawaii, I was packing books for Mari to take back to Florida for me. As I took Robert Monroe's newest book, *The Ultimate Journey* off the shelf to pack, I had a very strong sensation and an inner voice that said, "Now is the time." I had wanted to go there for over 10 years but the way never seemed to open. Now I was going back to the East Coast. I had lots of time and extra money from selling everything. The greatest of all was the motivation to make greater contact with you in the spirit world. His books had many stories of how he and many people that have taken the classes had made contact with deceased love ones. I thought how wonderful it would be if I could travel through those realms of inner space and have you as my guide.

I called them right away and found out they were booked six months ahead. I really didn't want to wait that long. The registrar told me to call her when I got to the East Coast and she would let me know if anything happened to open up.

While in Florida, the registrar called and said there were so many people that didn't want to wait they decided to add a whole class just for us. I thought wow, what a class. A whole group of us that manifested our own class. Again this was a lifesaver. I needed some excitement in my life. I was going to do something I had wanted to do for years. I love learning new things in this area, traveling through the spiritual realms and bringing back information. Having these spiritual adventures was a high for me. A whole week of intense, deep, inner searching and exploring. And now, most of all, hopefully making a stronger connection with you.

The class was called Gateway Voyage and was held in the foothills of the Blue Ridge Mountains in Virginia on hundreds of acres of quiet peaceful land. It consisted of 5-6 taped guided exercises a day. We heard Robert Monroe's voice through headphones combined with specific sound frequencies to assist us to go to levels that are beyond normal consciousness. They are meant to be tools to assist us to have a conscious out of body experience. The institute clearly states there are no guarantees. We listened to the tapes in these little curtained booths that also served as our bed.

He also wrote a book, *Journeys Out of the Body* that I had read in 1978. It is based on the belief that we are spirits temporarily occupying a physical body and we have the ability to leave that body at will and travel to other places on this planet or to other dimensions, like the many levels of what people call heaven. He had many such experiences, and reading his material had created a desire for me to learn to do so. Throughout the years, I have tried many different techniques. I remember for a while, right after reading the book, I had practiced a technique a friend of mine had used successfully. She said she would lie down on her bed and imagine herself getting up and walking to the door. Then she would imagine herself walk back to her bed and got in it. Then she would actually get up and do the same thing physically trying to trick her subconscious, until one time that she got up and went back to her bed and saw that her body was already in the bed. I tried the technique for a while but didn't persevere. One of the ways that people know that they are out of their bodies is when they can look back and see their body.

My dad once had an experience where he was feeling quite elated and fell asleep and then looked down and saw his body on his bed. He was so frightened by it that his spirit immediately returned to his body. It is quite common for people to get so excited or scared once they see them-selves that it catapults them back into their body. One of the keys is to be able to remain calm during that experi-ence. The first time I ever saw my body I felt thrilled. I had wanted to get out for such a long time. I also ended up right back in my body.

In Atlanta, in 1989, I took a class on traveling out of body with Gary Bonnell. He said that it was important to make peace with your body first before you could travel out of it. So many people do not want to be in their body. The body has to know that it will not be abandoned. His sugges-tion was to send love to it and appreciate it. Then the body will be more apt to let your spirit go. It was a good experi-ence for me to make some peace with my body, for at that time I didn't have a very good attitude towards it.

When Gary, who could read auras, first came up to me in the class he asked me where I had traveled. He had a clear sense that he could tell somehow I traveled out of body. I know I did visit many places in meditations, but was not sure it was considered an OOB (Out of Body experience). It seems that there are actually different kinds or levels of OOB's.

One of the techniques he taught was to roll back and forth inside your body from side to side. You would just use your imagination as a tool and visualize your spirit rolling to one side and then back to the other side. This worked quite well for me. I could actually feel myself outside my body.

Robert Monroe had a similar rolling technique, but just to one side. You would feel yourself rolling like a log, and just roll out of your body and then look back at your body after lifting yourself above it. I had difficulty with that part. I had only seen my body from above only once and that was on the way back in from a Ro-Hun session. It was a very powerful experience because I was able to view my body from a detached viewpoint and see what an absolute miraculous creation it was that God had created. I saw all the amazing things it could do. It was a powerful experience in healing my attitude towards accepting my body. I could see that even though it was not perfect in the way I thought it should be from a human point of view, that it was quite perfect from a spiritual point of view. I felt so grateful for my body after that experience. Grateful that I had arms, and legs, and eyes, and ears, and on and on. It just seemed like such an incredible piece of Gods' work. Now I see how peoples' bodies are perfect just for them, and fit them in some way.

Just like you honey, even though you were a little chubby around the waist I thought you were just perfect for you. I guess most bears seem kind of pudgy in the waist. You used to be afraid I would not find you attractive and I thought you were perfect just the way you were. Your spirit was so beautiful, it just shined through your body and made your body appear the same. I think when you love someone you just automatically also love his or her appearance.

Any way, back to going to the Monroe Institute, I pre- pared myself by getting a whole set of tapes to help me get used to going to the different levels. I was excited with the idea of going there and communicating with you in perhaps a deeper or stronger way than I had already been doing. The tapes were called the Gateway Experience and it consisted of 36 tapes that worked progressively to explore deeper levels of consciousness. I was eager to use the tapes and it helped to make the time go by faster as I was waiting for the class to come up. They also helped me to feel more prepared for the class.

In order to begin I had to memorize the Gateway affirmation to set my intention. I already knew from my healing work how important it is to set intention. I always taught my classes that intention overrides technique. So the intention was the realization we are more than our physical bodies and since our inner beings go beyond the physical world we create a desire to know more about that part of ourselves, that part that is made up of pure energy. Because if we break down our bodies to cells, to molecules, to atoms, to sub-atomic particles and so on we basically come down to pure energy and we want to know more about that energy, how we can use it, control it and expand it for our benefit and for the benefit of those who follow in our steps. It also places the intent to call upon the assistance of more evolved beings to assist in our explorations. Whenever I do my healings or readings, I call upon the higher beings for assistance and guidance. Of course I know now when I call upon these spiritual beings you quite often come in to assist and I am grateful for your presence.

Before the affirmation we create a box to put in all our concerns so they don't distract us during exercises. This we also would do before a Ro-Hun Session. The client would put all their thoughts and concerns up into a ball of light and we would send it off to return later with the intention the thoughts would be filled with light and more organized and not so bothersome.

Then, we do a powerful breathing exercise that I have similarly used in my yoga and meditation classes. I emphasize; change your breath – change your consciousness. This breathing technique is meant to charge one's energy field and to quiet one's thoughts. As soon as one slows down their breath the mind automatically slows down with it because the mind and breath are so linked. Robert also adds an inadvertant way of chanting the OM sound, which is quite common in yoga. In yoga we chant it to connect with the cosmic sound of the universe. In deep mediation quite often yogis will hear a long hum sound that could be translated as om, aum, or even amen. In the breathing exercise we are to vocalize "aaah," "oooh," and "uuum," sounds as we exhale. Which I think is great. Quite often I would explain certain sounds that have a meditative effect on our bodies rather than a particular meaning. In the breathing exercises we would imagine ourselves filled up with sparkling vibrant light. I loved all these exercises because I already had a reference point for most of what we were doing.

I meditated last night to the sound of OM on tape. I listened and allowed my mind to just let go. An experience of immense peace came over me as my mind expanded; it felt like a totally calm mountain lake, so still it reflected all that was around it. The OM would be a powerful exercise to work with on a regular basis.

Surrounding myself with a bubble of light was another great preliminary exercise. I have also done this exercise in some of my Tantra practices. After one fills themselves up with their own vibrant energy through the breath and the toning of the OM sound, one brings the breath up to the top of the head, called the crown chakra. When I meditate on this spot I feel myself at one with all that there is. I focus all that energy at the top of my head and direct the breath so energy flows out from the top of my head like a fountain. Then I allow it to gently flow around my body and back up through the bottom of my feet. Then I allow the energy to spiral down and back up inside me. I can feel myself as if I am pure energy and my energy is expanding and becoming more vibrant. That is a key to this work. The more lighter and finer energies we have the greater our experiences. This is working on the principle of resonance, which attracts other energies to me that are equal to the level I'm vibrating at or that have a higher energy. It is like the higher your energies are the higher the beings you will attract. The resonance principle works here on the earth plane also. Quite often, when I would counsel women who were looking for their soul mates, I would advise them to become like the person they would most want to attract.

All this was already so powerful I could just imagine what the rest of the tapes would be like. What I was learning was to go to different levels that were called focus levels and each one had a different purpose. There were ways to program daily patterns, receive guidance, use colors for healing, gain more energy, more techniques for floating out of the body, techniques for moving forward or backward in time and for getting important questions answered like what is my purpose. The tapes were phenomenal, a life training course in itself.

When I did finally go, I felt prepared. We started with many preliminary exercises, learning focus 10 which was called mind awake, body asleep, then focus 12, called expanded awareness. Focus 15, a popular one was called no time. Somewhere near midweek, we went to a place they called level 21, the level on which one is most likely to meet a deceased loved one. As I traveled through the levels I was real careful not to go and look for you. I felt if you would appear, then it wasn't something I had made happen.

I saw a whole group of light beings that I've seen often before in meditations, which I call the White Brotherhood. Then, behind one, I saw you peep out with a white hood over your head. You started to run toward me. I noticed your steps were heavy. There was a joyful reunion. I felt a lot of emotions and many tears of joy. It felt so good to strongly connect with your energy again. I was feeling an abundance of love, joy and ecstasy as our energies joined together. My heart was overflowing. And then the voice on the tape over the headphones I was wearing said it was now time to return. I felt like once again I was being separated from you. After four months, finally I found you and now I had to let you go again. I felt the pain of the separation return as I came back to normal consciousness. I cried and cried feeling the sadness of losing you again. It seemed unbearable.

Two hours later we were to do another taped exercise returning to the same level. My body was fidgety and my head ached. I heard intuitively that this was my body's resistance of re-experiencing the pain of the last session. Did I really want to go through that again? I breathed through it, asking for help, so I could find you again.

Finally, I moved up into focus 21, as they call it, and found you immediately. This time we did something with our energies to balance them out so we would not be so overwhelmed. You sat facing me guiding me to connect and harmonize our energies through our chakra centers. It was a way to meditate together to calm our spirits. There weren't really words spoken, just a beautiful, loving, harmonious and joyous energy exchange.

Then, I don't really remember how it happened, but the

scene changed. I was intuitively led to the right, through a series of arcs of lights on clouds. I had seen them the first time I went up, but I didn't go in that direction. This time I was led and I saw you lying on a table sleeping. I really didn't understand, but nonetheless I was happy to know where you were. I thought maybe I was supposed to wake you. I tried gently at first and then more strongly. You didn't wake up, so I kissed you and once again had to return with the voice on the tape. It was easier to leave this time. As I returned, I was strongly connected to you and felt I could reach up and touch you anytime I wanted. I would let you rest just as comfortably as if your were home and you wanted to take a nap.

When I returned to normal consciousness, we gathered as a group for a discussion. I expressed how I was happy to have found you, yet was a bit confused about how I had communicated with you and also how you were asleep. What I got was an intriguing possibility. On earth we can have communication with others while we dream. Here you were not even being in the physical and still communicating with me from a dream state on your level. We don't often think of spiritual beings napping.

I remember after my mom died, I tried everything I knew to find her and never seemed to connect, eventually giving up. I did dream about her and one time I received information from her about my dad that turned out to be true. Six years later I connected with her during a group psychic session in a spiritual development class I was taking at Delphi in the Georgia Mountains. A group of seven of us sat around in a circle in a dimly lit room at around 8 p.m. We were in a house in the mountains and you could hear the crickets outside and it felt as if they were sounding with anticipation. Three of us were taking turns on different evenings to contact our loved ones that had passed over for the purpose of healing. I was both excited and nervous. We held hands and put ourselves in a quiet meditative state by doing some deep breathing. I thought of a time that I had felt close to her and called out to her by the name I did when she was alive which was just mom. I used the love from my heart as a telephone line and at the same time one of the other women in the group helped call her in by saying her name, Lenore Martin, out loud three times. As we did that I could unmistakably feel her energy come in. It was more expansive and loving than what I had experienced on earth. I could tell the group could feel her and enjoyed feeling her energy. I was happy to introduce my mom to the group. She had always been a loving and generous presence to my friends. At first, everyone was just giving their impressions and I was saying yes, no or I don't know to confirm their information. Later, I spoke to her and told her I would be speaking to my father and what message could I give him from her. She told me to tell him that the ring he gave her meant a lot to her now and when he gave it to her. I had no idea what she was talking about but later when I asked my dad he said he knew that she meant the ring that he had made her when they were in high school in the metal shop class. This was another proof that we had indeed contacted her and my dad was happy to get the message. I also told her I had tried to contact her after she commented she had been trying to get through to me. It was at this point she told me that after she left earth she had taken a long rest. I also read that often beings sleep or take a rest period before starting their new life in the spirit world. So I didn't think it was strange that you would be sleeping.

I had a wonderful confirmation when we had the group discussion from the parents of a very gifted autistic child.

Their child is very psychic and communicates with them telepathically. She has guided them in many things on their spiritual path. The father asked their child where you were and she told him you were sleeping. This was a great confirmation for both of us on the information we were receiving inwardly.

During the rest of the week there wasn't any more contact with you, just a feeling of contentedness in knowing where you were.

(Afterlife)

Yes, Beloved, I remember getting tired and wanting to sleep. At first when I passed over, as you would say, it was exciting. It was just as if I had fallen asleep and woke up in a new place. You and I had traveled many times into these dimensions and they were very familiar to me. I was excited by this new place. You and I had never feared death and spoke about it often, so in a way I was prepared for it. My dad was there to meet me. You and I had discussed the expectation of a deceased loved one being there to meet us. It was very good to see him and my grandfather. There was a sense of immediate understanding of things that had been misunderstood on earth in our relationships. I didn't stay with my dad long. Once I was adjusted to what had happened and got reacquainted with other old friends; I went to a different location from my dad.

There was a concern with your distress. I kept trying to communicate to you that we would soon be together again, that you too would soon be here and not to take my death so hard. It was difficult with me feeling so good and you being so distressed. Eventually I decided I just wanted to rest as the excitement wore off and I kept watching you in pain. I was torn within myself. I had many exciting things happen as I was shown around. I learned so much of what I had forgotten on earth. At times I could feel you pull on me as you were trying to cope. I tried to comfort you as much as possible and then I just got tired. I wasn't really sleeping just resting, as I continued to get readjusted to my new environment, and to knowing the pain you were in as a result of my death. I was told you would be all right and get through it okay. You would just need a longer readjustment period than I would, and that it had been an agreement we had made before we went to earth. In one way that made it easier and in another way it was still difficult to feel you in such torment. So I took a rest, and I was still aware of you as I was resting.

(Sympathy vs compassion)

I am sorry, Bear. I could feel that it was difficult for you to deal with my sadness. I was so much into my own energy. I couldn't get out to realize the extent of how difficult it was for you. I suppose that might be one of the reasons why some cultures recommend one doesn't think of or mention the deceased one's name after death, so they do not pull on their energy. I don't know if I could have done anything different than I did. I had to go through those feelings. I suppose that is also one of the experiences of life: being able to stand by one that we love while they are going through a dark experience; being able to stand back and have compassion, without being brought down ourselves; knowing what they are going through is, in the long run, what will be best for them. Things are much better now. I have learned many valuable lessons that I will be able to use the rest of my earth life. My greatest lesson is the attitude of gratitude, to consciously take time to be grateful for life and the people in my life. Love is a precious thing. To have people in life to share that love with is something to be appreciated. Fighting is so much less important and can be such a waste of precious time, while being in the presence of the ones I love. To have a physical body and to be able to touch people is something to be appreciated. Not that I didn't know this before, but now these things have been so much more impressed upon my life. Sadness isn't something to be avoided but: a part of myself to be honored; to recognize its messages (in honor of what was joyful); to move through it and into higher levels of joy than have been experienced before.

Trusting in the universe that I am taken care of leads me where it is best for me to go, rising above all judgment. Being more compassionate to all beings even if I don't understand their behavior or situation - trusting each person is exactly where they need to be and not to take what may be a negative state of mind personally. Remembering others may be in challenging situations to learn their own valuable lessons.

It takes a lot of strength to be able to stand by and support someone. I want to give compassion without allowing their feelings to bring me down. I need to stay strong and centered and not feel sorry for them. There is no need to feel sorry for anyone. There are no victims in this world. All experiences, even those that seem bad, are in some way beneficial, but seldom clear in the moment. If I feel sorry for them, I support them in staying in a weak role, rather than finding their own source of strength and power to get through the challenges in life. Although I still love and support them, I want them to feel the reward through their sense of personal power in life. All human beings are connected to a great source of higher power, a higher part of themselves that is connected to God. It is from that point that we live our best lives.

I know for you, Bear, it was always difficult for you to see others suffer or feel sad. You yourself had been in the past one that tended to look to others for sympathy. Sometimes people confuse sympathy with love. You learned that in the long run it didn't benefit you. However, your tendency was to still feel sorry for others. I myself still, at times feel sorry for other's suffering, but when I lift above it, I can see the greatness of it all. So as it is with you, I feel sorry that I made it so difficult for you to have to watch me go through all this. I would hope that you could tap into your strength and higher vision to be strong yourself, as I go through my trials. I can try to be stronger for you and you can try to be stronger for me. Deal?

Thank you, Bee. Your wisdom and insight into life is so great. Your wisdom has always been an inspiration to me. What you have communicated to me, my friends have also communicated to me. Although I am here, I still have some residue of earth plane conditions that I am working through, because of my connection to you. Some beings that come here just move right on with their new life, but for me the agreement is to continue to have the opportunity to learn from the earth plane while I am still in transition from one dimension to another. Watching you go through your trials is an opportunity for me to see and to know at the same time that there are greater lessons happening. It creates a deeper impression in my consciousness that bad things do not really happen to people. All is really good and has its value in its own way. If people could see it from this point of view, they would know this truth. I can now see it much better from this viewpoint than I could when I was living on earth. I am now grateful for the

Thank you, bear. I am very happy to know that you have been able to see it from your greater perspective.

I was grateful for my experience with you at the Monroe Institute. When I left I had an anonymous gift of the Going Home series of tapes developed by Monroe and Elizabeth Kubler Ross and Charles Tart. I was quite surprised. The whole group was so supportive I had no idea who it could have been. The tapes were meant to help terminally ill people to release the fear of death by having the experience of going over to the other side. The tapes also helped the caregivers let go of their fear of having their loved ones die by also having experiences of where they went after death. It was based on focus 21. So I believe they were giving them to me so I could have more experiences of what it was like where you were and possibly more contact with you. I also signed up for another program that you had to be a graduate in order to take called guidelines. So I would be returning three months later.

Calling Back My Power

June 27

Hello beloved,

I've missed writing to you these last few days. Although I've felt you with me at times, it's not the same as when I write to you. I feel you more consciously over the extended period of time writing the letter.

There are so many things that still remind me of you. There is a movie out called "The Rock." I saw a movie the other day where a woman in a hospital watched as they tried to bring back her lover with those shocks to the heart - the similar scene that I watched as they worked on you in the hospital. Tears streamed down my face from mixed feelings of having compassion for her and remembering my own sadness. I think of you when I see people doing landscape work (which is all over here), or when I see someone who has a similar appearance to yours. I'm not really sure if there is a day that goes by that I still don't think of you.

I have done a lot of healing this year. I now have my normal energy back, and maybe even excess energy at times. I feel a real urge to go out and do my soul's work. I want to go back to teaching again, sharing what I have learned about life with others, including dancing with my soul. I am just not sure where I want to settle down yet.

I can feel I am right at the edge of the transition bridge and I am being patient and trusting during the last few steps.

Gathering my energy back to me from afar...

Feeling the lightness of my soul

and calling in the joy.

The call to manifest joy...

I call to manifest joy,

To move from the depths to the heights...

To refill.

Deeper you go more space to refill...

Bringing in abundance with the joy...

Centering into a place of peace and balance...

Dancing and trancing,

With spirit moving me.

Living on the earth in joy!

See above the judgment...

Rising above duality.

Seeing the soul above the body,

remembering it's just a dream.

In the dream there is a sadness,

in the soul there is the joy.

Wake up from sleeping

and experience the soul.

Moving through Fear

August 10

Hello, my dear beloved,

So good to be with you again. How many times can I say how grateful I feel that you're still a part of my life? I drove from Georgia to Florida and am temporarily visiting my sister in Cocoa Beach. Her and her husband have a magnificent four bedroom home right on the water. I see the dolphins and sunsets regularly from the back deck. I also am close enough to walk to the beach. I love walking on the long flat beaches here.

I can still relive the times of joy, like our wedding day. I bought the CD the other day with the Hawaiian Wedding Song by Andy Williams. I know you hear it and can feel me when I play it. The first time I heard it, my stomach got all tight. It reminded me on some level of the memory of the pain associated with the song. I shared it with Mari. The more and more I played it, the easier and easier it became to hear.

I recall when I was five years old and my mother drove down an elevator shaft in a New York City parking garage. The car dropped one floor with us in it. After that, I was so afraid whenever I was in a car driving down a hill. I remember everyone laughing at me, because I would plead with them to let me out to walk. I am sure, subconsciously, I was afraid of hitting bottom again. Eventually, after having to go down so many hills, I got over the fear. Although, to this day I certainly do not like roller coasters or ferris wheels.

When we fear something, a way to gain our power back, is to find a way to move through the fear. Quite often that would mean repeating a similar situation with the realization it does not have to have the same outcome. I sense deep within me that I have some fear now of getting married again and losing a second husband. I have met other women who have lost more than one husband. The fear isn't

great enough to stop me, but it does exist. It actually dimin-
ishes as time goes on.

(Money)

My darling Bee,

You're so beautiful Bee. How wonderful to see and feel your energy close to me again. How much I adore you, as I watch you walk along the beach, the sun shining on you as the ocean waters caress your feet. I feel our love and our connection. I feel grateful for the love that we share. Yes, for me, here, I know it will only be a short while before you will be here. We can then share stories of our adventures on the planet earth. You will be laughing a lot with me. I must admit there are things that we thought were so meaningful but really had nothing of lasting value, like money; from here I can see how foolish it was for me to be so concerned about money. Remember the times I would get so depressed about paying taxes. From here, I can see how in many ways some of my values were not in the best order.

Since the day I met you there was a deep part of me that knew the value of having you in my life. It was what got me through our challenging times. Oh, Bee, our love is even stronger than we had imagined when we were on earth.

The energy on the earth is dull compared to the energy here. That is a reason why we want to lighten the earth's energy. You have been getting intuitive feelings and thoughts recently about desiring things, like certain foods, that give you more energy. It is a part of our work, clearing up the energy. There are many different ways for people to contribute. Your contribution is to first do it yourself and then be an example to others who also start to feel the impulse.

Other Relationships

My beloved Rock,

My dear, as you know, I've been resisting writing recently. It's because I wasn't sure how or if I should. I do feel I need to write this to get it out. It's the topic of another relationship. After you died, I thought I would never be able to be with another man again. You had been so wonderful and so right for me that no one would be able to measure up to what we had. Also, I still felt married to you. I still felt I was your wife and you were my husband.

About five months after your death, I reconnected with an old friend of mine, Roy, during my travels. His presence was very comforting to me as he listened to the stories of my experiences with you. I also comforted him as he shared some of his personal challenges. I often spent time at his house during my travels through Europe and up and down the East Coast. The idea of a new relationship really frightened me. Slowly and gently over the next eight months I was able to move through the fear.

What helped greatly was a message I received in meditation. Clearly this relationship was a gift being offered from the universe. I could either stay fearful and walk away, or go through my fear and receive the gift of healing.

I wasn't concerned because of you. In fact, while I was with him, I felt your presence and your approval of the whole situation. One might think that you would have been upset or have a similar reaction, as if you had still been here. It wasn't like that at all. You were very supportive. You knew that even if I did get more involved, it didn't affect our love in any way and you were right. Caring for someone else does not take away from the love you and I share.

There was another challenge for me to face, and that was the judgment of others or by society about me getting involved in a relationship so soon after your death. It really goes back to what I keep getting over and over again. We have no right to judge another's circumstances. We really don't know what path others are meant to walk. I was a little nervous about the reaction first, of my family. My family has pretty much always been supportive of me in whatever my decisions have been. None the less, I had to call each member of my family and let them know I was bringing a guest with me to our Christmas reunion.

After my mom had died, my dad had a similar situation. He connected with a woman who had been a friend and a business acquaintance. They ended up getting together very soon after my mom's death. When I told my dad about Roy, he thought it was a great idea. Roy's family was also supportive.

There were other people whom we would meet up with where I could just feel the judgment. Eventually, I got over it and didn't care anymore what people thought. I knew deep in my heart I was led to be involved in this relationship. Their judgment comes from their limited knowledge.

I also have a wonderful aunt who met her recent husband at the funeral parlor. He had lost his wife at the same time she lost her husband. She also had to face a lot of judgment from others. But now she has been very happily married to this man for over fifteen years.

My relationship with Roy still had its ups and downs, like any relationship. There were times when I felt you there reminding me how I needed to be patient. You guided me through some of my challenges. I started to get stronger and stronger from all the healings that had taken place on my travels. It was getting more difficult for me to stay at Roy's because of its seclusion. I was getting my energy back and I needed to channel it in some way that would be joyful. I felt the need to be more social. Also, after spending all that money traveling, I needed to increase my financial situation. My spirit was giving me intuitive feelings that I needed to return to my sister's in Florida. The longer I tried to hold off, the more frustrated my energy became. So with a sad good-bye, I left, trusting my intuition was guiding me where I needed to be.

So here I am, and my spirit is much lighter now. I love being near the beach and in the warm sunshine. I am around people more often. I am writing to you and computerizing everything. It feels so right to be here. It is amazing how my spirit tells me when I need to move on. If I don't follow my feelings, my energy gets all tied up. I am less and less unable to follow my truth. When I am not following my truth, my energy gets repressed and sometimes I get sick. I am not able to do much of anything, or the messages very clearly impress me not to do it again.

My relationship with Roy obviously had not been much like ours. You and I never wanted to be apart. Roy and I did better when we had more space, time and distance in the relationship. The choice of our lifestyles was very different. It didn't work if we spent a whole lot of time together.

In retrospect, I would say that the relationship really allowed a healing for me to get over the fear of another relationship. We had a previous trust built up. He had a level of sensitivity that allowed me to move through the fear. This allowed me to be stronger in my life, since fear only weakens. I can see now it was not meant to be a long lasting relationship.

I can also see that when someone loses a mate, many different situations may come up for people. The popular psychological viewpoint is that one should not boomerang from one relationship to another, because one may be in a weakened and vulnerable state of mind. People should realize this, but also each of our situations are unique. We each need to remain aware of our own situation and pay attention to what our own inner voice leads us to do.

I am grateful for the time I had in this relationship: for the healing I received; for the healing I was able to give; for the things I learned about myself; for the strength I gained; for the love I was able to share with him and his family; for the time I was able to have in the healing room we created; and for all the Trance Dancing I was able to do there.

No Time

August 15

Hi, honey,

I was so excited today. While I was walking on the beach, I was contemplating your experience of no-time. My sister and I had been discussing the topic yesterday. I was wondering how it was not to have a sense of time. So today, I was feeling really good as I was breathing fresh sea air, walking on the long flat beach with the warmth of the sunshine on my body. I was feeling myself being energized by the sun and my breathing. My heart was open and I was feeling quite happy.

I was doing some deep, conscious breathing. I felt blissful and peaceful. I was acutely aware of all my surroundings. My senses were so filled with the beauty of nature that I had no sense of time. There was just the space I was in. I envisioned you living in this space, knowing soon I would be there. Soon implies a sense of time but I know no other word to use.

It was such a pleasant state to be in. Life on earth would be much more enjoyable if one could achieve those states of consciousness more often. The neat thing was that I had wanted to know what it must be like for you to live in the dimension without a sense of time. I can see how things must be more peaceful, because there isn't the stress of hurrying around to get things done. It is amazing how much we live our lives here according to the watch. Even though I experienced spaces of no-time on the beach, I had to move back into time, because my car was parked at a meter. If I lost track and got there late, I could get a ticket.

I know it is necessary and beneficial for us to have time here. Things can be slowed down. We can focus in on parts of our lives, to give some attention to details that can help our evolution. Today I also realized how often I have experienced no-time periods. It can happen easily in a rhythmic activity like walking, if one doesn't allow the thoughts to interfere.

I have recently joined a wonderful watercolor class. I did it spontaneously because I knew I would love it. I had been yearning to do some art. I had bought some more oils but never took them out. I figured I could use some of what I learned in this class and also apply them to oils. It would be valuable to learn another medium. I had never really had much training in art, but have always loved it.

In art class I always experience no-time. It is a three-hour class. The only way I know it is time to leave is when I see other people start to clean up. In that sense, I experience living in no-time. I am so engrossed and really enjoy what I am doing. I enjoy the experience of no-time and the fact that my thoughts are not coming in and interrupting my experience. I believe now, I experience no-time more often then I was aware of. Now, I will become more aware of it.

I remember when I went to Egypt for a spiritual gathering called the 11:11 in 1992, the facilitator shared with us a technique to program no-time. I also remember it when I was training to be a Silva Mind Development Instructor. They called it stretching time.

For example, if one was running late, one would picture oneself arriving on time instead of rushing and worrying about being late. I played with the concept a few times but never did it enough to say I mastered it.

I still think of you often throughout the day as things or people remind me of you. Yesterday, I must have seen about three or four guys with long, brown hair and a beard like you. Today I saw a few different landscape guys, doing lawns or driving in their trucks. It seems like reminders of you are constantly around me.

Today, I thought of you again on the beach. I was walking and was testing to see if I could communicate with the cloud beings to move off the sun so I could feel its' warmth. They were happily dancing across the sky making such lovely images. One reason why I was wanting to communicate with them was because I had been working on doing clouds in my art class today. I thought of you because of the time you and I visited them in our meditative travels into the spirit realm. I remember the technique I had heard many times on trying to make a hole in the clouds, using the power of the mind. Remembering the love I felt from them before, I re-connected with the cloud beings. I asked for confirmation of our connection by allowing a space to open in a certain area. It did open up!

I also realized their sense of time was much different than ours. On earth, there quite often seems a tendency to want to rush things. I could feel there was no rushing this situation. It would be more beneficial to just feel their depth of being, and merge with them, instead of trying to make it happen; it was more like allowing it to happen. It took some patience on my part. Then it was as if they wanted to play with me and guess what forms were being shaped. After a while, I got kind of bored with the game and moved my thoughts elsewhere.

Well, my dear beloved one, that is all for now. I will write again soon.

Much love to you, dear.

Your beloved Loryn

Symbolism of the Tarot

Aug. 18

Hello, my beloved husband,

I had a beautiful two-hour walk on the beach today. I've been doing a lot of creative visualization lately. I also have been playing with the tarot cards a lot. I love playing with them. They have so much wisdom and they really help to get a spiritual viewpoint about what is happening in my life. It is unfortunate that people have had bad experiences with some of the old gypsies. The cards can be read at all different levels. So one just has to make sure they get a reading from a reputable person.

Today, I worked on taking the eleven most important things I wanted to create in my life, and used the tarot card symbols to assist in my visualizations.

I used The Magician, card number one, to symbolize health. The Magician takes the energies of the universe and uses his mind to create with it. I use that energy to create divine health and energize my body.

Along with the divine health, I used my creative visualization for my weight control technique I first learned in Silva. Years before I met you I had always felt I had a problem with my weight. It took up much of my concern and self-esteem, until I finally applied this technique. The mind is truly powerful if we apply it. I just kept visualizing myself looking the way I wanted to look, but it did take a lot of mental control. I feel very confident that I will not have to battle a weight problem anymore. I realize that my weight tends to go up and down within that six pound range, but I don't worry when I begin to gain weight, because I know I can, and will drop it again.

The second is the High Priestess. She works inward with her intuition. She has more connection with the inner forces and inner guidance. I use her as my visualization for a stronger connection with your world, the spirit world. I want stronger inner guidance and stronger communication with you. I want my inner vision opened so I can see you rather than just sense you.

The third is the Empress, also known as the Divine Mother. She is connected with abundance. I use this symbol for abundance on all levels. It includes a greater connection with the abundance of nature, beauty, and finances.

Fourth is the Emperor, who has a strong sense of power in his life. He knows his ability to be an authority in his own space. With him, I saw myself feeling a strong sense of self.

The Emperor lead me to the fifth, which is the Heirophant. This is my destiny number, by adding up my birthdate. He is the teacher of truth, which is my path. I visualized myself teaching and sharing the truths that have been helpful to me during challenging times.

The sixth is the card of the Lovers. It quite often means a choice. I used this symbol for living in this world with an open heart. I used the feeling of the blissful union I had in a vision with you during a Trance Dance experience when I saw myself unite with you in an explosion of love, after my death. I brought that experience into my heart to make it a reality now.

The Chariot, number seven, represented going forth, having accomplishments that are in alignment with my purpose.

The Strength card is number eight. It has an astrological association with the sun. So I used the Sun to symbolize the joy and enthusiasm that I seek in life.

The ninth card is the Hermit, the one that goes inward, also represented by the wise old woman. I used it with the moon card to symbolize going into the dream world. I want to go into my unconscious and become aware of my dreams, their significance and any other patterns that would be of benefit to bring into the light. I enjoy discovering new parts of myself.

The tenth card is the Wheel of Fortune. I used the World card with this one. It has a dancer on the front of it signifying my destiny and my fortune to dance freely and joyfully through life. I also want to continue dancing with people from all over, energizing the planet as we do so.

The eleventh is the card of Justice. It has the woman sitting on a chair with a scale in one hand and a sword in the other. I used the Judgment card with this card to symbolize strengthening my ability to see people from the viewpoint of their souls, to see the higher purpose in all the experiences. I understand why they use angels in that card, because it is like having the viewpoint of an angel. One does not judge, but rises above judgment.

A real neat thing happened today as I was walking on the beach. I was remembering how on the beach in Hawaii, you used to love to find pretty shells and give them to me. I would think they were so pretty and would love the gesture of you finding and giving me such a gift of nature. I would bring them home and add them to my collection, some of which I still have. While I was walking on the beach, in this state of mind, this young man comes walking up to me and says (after startling me), "Isn't this a neat shell?" and handed it to me as a gift. I said thank you and continued walking. I thought of you and wondered if it was a gift from you. I suppose it could have been easy for you to suggest to him to give me a shell. Well, that is how I took it, as a gift from you. I brought it home with me to add to my shell collection. Thank you, my love, for the gift.

I must go now to meet my sister at the restaurant. I love you, Bear, and am more and more excited about our continued communication. Thank you for your love.

Your beloved wife, Loryn

Manifesting

August 19

Hello, dear one,

I just finished looking through our wedding pictures. They are my treasures of the memories of our wedding day and of the happiness of our relationship.

I worked again today on my visualizations and am excited about starting to see them manifest. I thought about how we started to manifest things as soon as you learned how to do it. I remember how challenging it was for me in the beginning of our relationship, because you had little knowledge of the power of the mind. I had to show you the possibilities. Frustration always shows up when I do not use my energies to create my life. Since our relationship was a partnership, I felt strongly we had to create together. Two energies are so much stronger than one, especially when it is enhanced by a love like ours. I feel there is a certain time in our life where we can create consciously. Up until then we are creating, but doing it unconsciously. People manifest things all the time in their life with their thoughts and don't realize it, because they are not aware of their thoughts. I learned about manifesting mostly from the Silva Mind Development Course when I was 19, which turned my life around. It gave me so much confidence in my life by testing and using the power of positive thinking. It sounds real easy, and on one level it is. On another level there is a lot to learn. I used to believe I could just think about something and it would happen, and sometimes it does; but most of the time a lot of energy has to be put behind the thought with clear intention.

For us, the most powerful example was when we decided we were going to manifest a boat. We had so little money and it seemed impossible, but we just went for it. We did what some call eat, drink and sleep boat. For one month we focused on boats, boats, and more boats. We went down to the harbor and watched the boats, dreaming of what it would be like when we owned a boat. We read all the classified ads on boats, and went to look at some of them. Every time we saw a boat for sale on the side of the road, we would stop and look at it. We were just so focused on boats and how much fun we would have owning a boat. We did what creative visualization calls for: strong desire; belief in the possibility, visualizing how it would look; and feeling the joy of going out on the boat. We both imagined doing what we loved to do. You saw yourself making some money fishing and I envisioned myself swimming with dolphins. Three months later we had manifested a boat under amazing circumstances.

After that, you were convinced of the power of visualization and your confidence increased. You saw you had more power to create your life than you had realized. What amazed me was the house we moved into three months before your death. It was exactly how you had described your dream house. It was a wooden house with a cabin- like feel to it, with a fireplace and a loft. For me I dreamed of a place with lots of acreage and no neighbors, so we could have quiet surroundings.

When our landlords first notified us they were ready to

sell the house we were living in, you were very upset. You really enjoyed that beautiful new house with low rent. The view of the ocean from the deck was spectacular. Hawaii is known for its splendid sunsets and the view from our deck was the best!

I was ready for a move. I was feeling cramped because of living so close to the neighbors and sound traveled so easily. I disliked it when I heard our neighbors screaming at each other. Sometimes it sounded like the man hit his girlfriend. It was so difficult for me to hear that go on and not do anything.

You changed your viewpoint quickly when we found another house to rent within a month. I remember when we first went up to see where it was located, we were in shock. We thought we must have the wrong house. It was just what you wanted. It was a beautiful cedar home with a fireplace and a loft. I was amazed. Of course I loved the fact that it was on five acres of property and behind us were acres and acres of pasture land, with not a neighbor in sight. And to top it off, the rent was even less than the other house. Even though I believe in the powers of the mind to manifest, I still get excited when I see it happen. It was your dream house and we got to live in it the last three months of your life.

As usual, you showed the ability to learn a concept and master it quickly. I remember a strange experience I had when I first met you. You really weren't into any other of the metaphysical arts at all, only recently a friend of yours had introduced you to the Chakra system. It's not a term that is familiar to most people here in the West, but once it is explained, it is fairly easy to understand the basics and how it applies to our lives. You having that as a basis of information helped me to communicate to you what my field of study was. Normally, I would not even have gotten involved with a man who didn't have a spiritual background, but I was getting such strong intuitive feelings about you. And this experience lead me to a new understanding.

Because of my healing background, sometimes it is second nature for me to just want to touch someone when they are in need of healing. This quite often just means they need extra energy to get back in balance. You were not feeling well, so I put my hand on your heart, explaining to you how I was visualizing a channel of energy moving through me. I was imagining a faucet of energy turned on over my head, connecting with Divine Energy, and breathing energy from the top my head, through my heart into you. This idea you could pretty readily accept. As I was energizing you through your heart, it was as if a vision of you on a higher level came into my mind. I could feel you had such a beautiful heart energy, meaning it wasn't shut down or closed as are some peoples'. It was as if another part of you was communicating something that was very important for me to understand. I was getting a lot of psychic impressions about you and your life, insights that you were confirming for me as I was expressing to you what I was picking up. It allowed me to get to know you on an inner level very quickly, parts of you that might have taken me months to get to know. The most impactful piece of information I received was that indeed you really were a very spiritual-type person, even if you hadn't studied any of the things that I had. I also got that you needed the space to learn things in your own way. You were not one to commit to any type of structural learning unless necessary. That is the best way to explain what I saw and heard. It was quite an unusual experience for me to have, but it helped me to accept you as a partner much more readily. It turned out to be very true and a very helpful piece of information. I needed to give you the space to learn things in your own time. My natural energy is one of a teacher. I tend to want to teach, and with you I had to pull back my energy and not be so much of a teacher or a healer, unless you asked. I needed to give you lots of space which wasn't always very easy. I could see how much benefit you and I would receive if you had certain pieces of information and applied them. But as you kept reminding me, I needed to be patient with you. That is a major lesson in my life.

Rising Above Judgment

August 25

Dear Bear,

I am visiting some friends and going through a very challenging time. Here lives an old lady, Agatha, who is very difficult to please. When I first got here, I felt sorry for her because she complained a lot that no one had talked to her. She was feeling sorry for herself, and obviously was not happy in her life. Compared to many people her age, she has good health. She overcame cancer and lost her second husband to death, which of course I can relate to. But she is very critical and sees the negative in most things. When I first got here, her main activity was watching soap operas and other TV shows most of the day, cleaning the house in between. When she did talk, it was always about the bad things on the news or in the paper. She rarely spoke an encouraging word to anyone, except maybe the dog. Once we started to get more acquainted she began to tell me; how she thought I should dress; wear my hair; how all the health food products I bought were a waste of my money; and when the dog needed to go out for a walk. I tolerated her even though I felt as if I were back under parental domain, even though 37 seemed a little too old for that. I saw how she yearned for some attention. I never saw her affectionate or nurturing.

I tried to do things the way she wanted them, but it just became impossible. It seemed there was no way I could do everything the way she wanted me to. She is a fanatic about cleanliness and no one could ever do anything well enough in her eyes. I know this is just a defense that people use to make themselves feel better, by making others look bad. After a while she stopped talking to me whenever I visited. I would say hello and she would be silent. So I stopped trying.

This woman was filled with judgment and criticism. I knew that I was being scrutinized and there would always be something I would do that she would find as wrong. I had to learn how to live under a judgmental energy being thrown at me almost constantly. It was quite a switch for me. She really went overboard. She hid the coffee, the filters, the toilet paper, the saran wrap and the aluminum foil. If I used the drying towel in the kitchen, she would change it. If I put my tomatoes on the counter, she moved them to the other side. She threw out some of my expensive vitamin products and then denied doing it. She had to move everything. There was not a thing that I put on the counter that she didn't move. I am not really sure why, I guess she felt she had a better sense of control. But after awhile it became a joke to see how long and where something we put on the counter would be moved. My friends have an enormous amount of patience with her. But then again, they are not around much.

Obviously, she is there for me to learn lessons from. My friends tolerate her because she is an old friend of the family and has no place to live. She had already been kicked out of three of her family members' houses.

I knew it was a test for me and I would have to rise above it. I remembered my desire to move back into the state of consciousness I had achieved once briefly while in the Atlanta airport, which is a state I desire to achieve more often. The awareness to see above things, above judgments, seeing the world as a stage and we are all players in a play. And this woman isn't the wicked witch of the East as she portrays, but really is a spiritual being temporarily living on the earth, forgetting who she really is in order to learn some earth lessons. My part in it isn't to judge her, but to see it as if she is purposely in my life for a time period, and to discern what value I can receive out of what seems like a negative condition. When I do that, there are numerous values I receive.

Probably the first and foremost is not to judge others. Her life is so miserable because she sees everyone else as wrong, instead of giving people the space to be different from what she thinks is right or proper. I, at times, use her way of being as a catalyst for prayer to God to help me to rise above judgement. We can use our ability to discern, which in my opinion is to make a judgment without criticizing someone else. Also, I believe the more we get in touch with our intuitive selves, the less apt we are to criticize others. Our inner voice reminds us that we all have our own roles to play.

The amazing thing is that even the Bible says 'judge not, lest ye be judged', yet our religious wars are based on judging the other as the bad guy. I believe it is an exalted accomplishment for us as human beings to have our vision and our hearts open enough to live on this planet with more acceptance, tolerance, patience, and compassion. It doesn't seem like an easy task. I am sure it begins with being that way towards ourselves. Thus living here with this woman has motivated me to pray harder and more deeply to live above judgment and more into compassion.

She also motivates me to want to live on my own again in my own place. I am very grateful for my friends opening their home to me, and it is a beautiful house near the beach. After your death, I needed to be near people. But now I am much better, and she is a sign that I am not meant to stay here. Her energy tells me not to settle in. I would consider her behavior a sign that this is not a place to consider home. Home to me is a sacred place, where I need beauty, space, and peace. And I am now well motivated to find a new place of my own, in order to have all those things.

She also is a reminder of what it is like when someone

speaks sharply. For when she speaks now, it is only when she blows up and speaks with a lot of anger. It reminds me of when I have done the same and I pray to be mindful. In fact, many things she does remind me of when I have acted similarly, perhaps not to the extreme, but in a similar manner. I believe the universe is teaching me through an exaggerated mirrored reflection of my own behaviors. I have seen that happen before. In fact, you and I used to joke around about how it seemed we were mirroring each other. That was why you bought me that little hand mirror as a gift (and a joke). Ha, Ha, funny, funny.

She is a reminder for me to pray for her and not judge her. If I judge, then I am behaving in the same manner as her. And believe me, there have been many temptations to hide things and move things, to give her a taste of her own medicine. I realize that I would then be acting like her which is not what I want. When I rise above, I see a very lonely woman with a closed heart, no love in her life, no one to touch her, or hug her or feel that there are people around that care. She doesn't realize this is her own doing. What a miserable life to live, so cold hearted, only having the lives of the soap operas to look forward to. I know there are many things she could do to change the quality of her life, but she chooses to live as she lives. I really have no idea what her higher lessons are. I can just have compassion and use her as a reminder to live with a grateful heart.

She is one that teaches me there are people who do not want to know. There are people who prefer to live with the benefits of living an unhappy life. They enjoy getting sympathy from others by telling them how miserable everyone treats them; then they don't have to change. She also teaches me I am not meant to go in and save the world, but to help and assist others who want to change and grow. Everyone has their own free will and I am learning to step back, keep my mouth shut and allow others to be how they choose to be, understanding everyone has their own lessons to learn in their own time.

Well, dear one, thanks for listening. It has helped me to write this through and discuss my own personal challenges.

Much love, Loryn

Living in Disapproval

August 26

Hi, honey,

I've been thinking a lot today about the situation I wrote about yesterday. I know it's not good to focus on negative energy because what we focus on we attract. However, I must admit it's a real challenge for me. I can understand it from a higher level and yet I still catch myself being bothered by it quite often.

Living in the house with Agatha causes me to not want to be here, and yet at the same time I am grateful for my friends who so warmly invite me here. I feel better when I am out, and it reminds me of when I lived with my parents. I never wanted to be home because I felt scrutinized. I keep feeling afraid I will do something wrong and she will yell at me. I so dislike being yelled at, even though all I do now is ignore her when she blows up. My past pattern would be to yell or argue back. I have changed my pattern, but I still must deal with the negative energy being thrown at me. I do believe that is one of the reasons I have to go through this right now; to build up a resistance to negative energy. In the past it has been one of my weak points, especially since I have such a high level of sensitivity to energy. That was why I moved out of my family's house after graduating high school; I didn't like to be around everyone arguing and bickering all the time. There tends to be a lot of that going on with five children in the house.

Remember when I worked in sales and the one sales person, Marta, started really getting on my case. She was accusing me of things I didn't do and gave me a hard time. I know it was because she didn't like the fact I was so close to her in being the top salesperson. Everyone knew she cheated a lot because she got caught; but she kept accusing me of doing the exact thing she was doing. I felt deeply hurt. One day I went outside and cried, because I couldn't take all the verbal and psychic attacks. I knew she was showing me a very weak part of myself. Even then, I tried to pull my energy up, rise above it, and have compassion for her.

Marta actually has some similar patterns as Agatha. I remember one day Marta told us of this man who was stalking her at work. He started doing minor damage to her car. She probably didn't realize that perhaps she was doing something to provoke these events. Honey, I think back and I know I could deal with her much more effectively now. I know one day I will look back and see how ridiculous it was to allow Agatha to get to me. I mean, so what if she yells at me. Time does give us the opportunity to heal all.

I do think about what it must have been like for people who were in prisoner of war camps. They always had to be on alert for someone to come in and shoot them down. I know my issue is nowhere as bad as that, but for me, it means to always be aware and alert, and to be okay with living in disapproval.

Working in the metaphysical field leaves me open for quite a bit of judgment. Yoga was much less accepted when I started to teach it in 1980 than it is now. I even remember going into a church for a Sunday Mass and the priest was talking against yoga. That is what makes up much of our life here, the differences, and dealing with the differences. I suppose just as long as I know in my heart what is right for me, that is all that matters. People will always have different opinions.

I remember when I was participating in a workshop, we had to ask 20 people what they thought about how well each of us were participating by a simple yes or no. I would say a good 70% said I was and 30% said I wasn't. What I realized is they really had no idea because they couldn't see inside me. There were people who could appear to be participating but not really going to deeper levels. The other thing to realize is how I felt when someone said no. It took a conscious energy not to let their opinions affect me. I have a friend and mentor who used to say, "it is none of my business what others think of me." That's what I try to keep telling myself.

Power

August 27

Hi, Bear,

Well, I got lots of inspirations on the beach today. Actually, I do every time I go to the beach, but today I wrote things down so I would remember. When I take long walks, so many ideas come to me and I don't always remember them. It is so important for me to go and spend time on the beach. The sunshine always makes me feel more energetic and the ocean water cleanses me with its salt. The long walks allow me to breathe lots of fresh air and get some exercise. Walking also gives me contemplative time to do creative visualizations for manifesting. Plus I feel so nurtured by the ocean and so abundant having free leisure time.

The two to three hours I spend on the beach allows me time for deeper reflection.

The inspiration today was that I needed to go deeper into myself for writing. I needed to write things that I didn't want anybody to know, because I was afraid of their judgment. Power is revealed through the doorway of fear!

I remember when I was young, my mom bought me a diary for a gift. She told me never to write anything I wouldn't want anyone to know because someone might find it and read it. Since then, it seems I unconsciously hold that fear and I am very conscious of what I write. Actually it happened one time when an old boyfriend went through my papers while I was away. He saw some old writings to a previous boyfriend. It didn't go over too well. So there has been this block about writing very private things down, afraid somehow I will get in trouble for it. But it seems the whole theme lately is about rising above judgment, both mine and that of others.

On the beach today, I intuitively felt I needed to write about those real private matters, those that had been a great challenge and deeply personal for me.

The one thing that also came up for me was recalling my

panther. Remember when one night I played the drum and did a guided meditation for you to find what is called your power animal in the Shamanic tradition. I had gotten my power animal in a guided meditation about 1 1/2 years before I met you and never really used it. You had such a connection with animals I thought you might enjoy the experience. Well you certainly did! Your power animal was an ape. It had the qualities of being strong yet gentle, only being aggressive if bothered, and very protective of its family. After that, you bought the t-shirt of an ape and hung it on the wall of our bedroom. And of course, apes love bananas.

Today, the panther came to me in my mind while walking on the beach. In the Shamanic tradition they say if you don't connect with your animal often, you can lose it or it will go away. I interpret that as: if you don't stay conscious of it, it won't be of much use. I used it for protection a month ago when I was walking on the beach late at night. I wanted to enjoy a nice long, moonlit meditative walk. But I wasn't sure if it was safe or not. I used to do it quite often when I was a teenager in New Jersey. So how I did it was to see, sense, and feel my panther walking beside me. By using my panther for courage, I was able to have a more peaceful walk. They say most attack victims are ones that would seem easy prey. If I am walking strong with no fear, I'm less apt to be picked on.

Another time the panther came in handy was when I was in Virginia and my car had broken down. I was doing a lot of walking which I loved to do anyway. I was walking down the street and a dog came at me barking, quite obviously wanting to protect what it considered the boundaries of its territory. I felt myself afraid for a second because I didn't know how far the dog was going to pursue me. Out of nowhere, my energy shifted and I became real strong and I growled back at the dog telling it to get away. I was quite surprised at myself. I felt very strongly that it was the energy of the panther that moved through me to scare that dog.

When I first heard of the Shamanic art of working with animals, I never thought it would be something I would be interested in. It seemed like a lower world. My focus was going to the higher worlds where the Masters like Jesus, etc. and the angels reside. It was my favorite place to go. I couldn't understand why anyone would want to go into the animal world. Now I understand much more deeply. As human beings there is a part of us that is animal, even in our brains. To have the courage, speed and strength of a panther is fantastic. The panther teaches me many things.

All animals have something to teach us. Each have unique talents. I believe many people learn things from their domestic animals whether they realize it or not. At that time I never liked the picture of the ape on the T-shirt you hung up on our bedroom wall. It really didn't blend in with the decor. But now, after I have gotten more deeply into Shamanic work, I love the shirt and the ape. The ape has come to me in times where I needed physical strength.

I first met up with the panther again when I got back into doing Shamanic work while in Europe. In my Shamanic journey, I climbed on the panther's back and we ran through the forest; I could feel the strength of her body as she ran. Its speed and strength just awed me. She showed me how she could run through the forest totally focused on where she wanted to go and get there with tremendous speed. There are things I can move through fast, like learning things for personal growth, but there are other things I drag out. This panther was showing me ways I could move through more things with focus and speed. Somewhere I learned that to do things consciously you have to do them slowly. That is not the case. We can do things consciously and quickly. So in a way it was changing a thought pattern that would be beneficial for me in the future.

Even though the ape is not a power animal of mine, he has assisted me a few times in some tight spots. There was an exercise I was doing in a class that demanded a lot of physical strength. My mind kept suggesting I wasn't going to be able to get through it. Then a vision of the ape came in, along with some strange noises. The sounds relayed an understanding why it is helpful for people to grunt when lifting heavy weights. My energy was changed to great strength. I was like a witness watching the whole thing, amazed at what I was doing. It is like the story of the mother who raised the car off her child and never realized how she did it. She just did it without thinking. We know the mind has tremendous powers.

The other time the ape came in and assisted was when I was in the airport in Holland and was running late. The bags I was carrying were heavy, making it very difficult for me to run. I felt the strength of the ape, as if he were super imposed over me. It was like he was carrying the bags, making it easier for me to rush to catch the plane. I didn't pre-plan or call him, he just popped up to help. I was very grateful. I have a great love for monkeys and apes now; in fact, I have a great love for a lot more animals now because of all my Shamanic experiences. I used to be afraid of snakes and now I'm not. It doesn't mean I am not cautious, but at least I have touched one now. I have felt the intense power of the snake and can now understand why people enjoy them.

Giving a massage with the snake energy is sensually enjoyable. The snake moves so slowly, feeling every inch as it crawls. There is a lot of power in going ever so slowly and remaining totally aware each moment. Now that I write about it, I can see how the panther and the snake represent two speeds that both have their usefulness at different times. The snake also waits before it jumps or hisses. It doesn't automatically attack someone. It waits until the timing is perfect. But if you come too close, it will let you know you'd better not come any closer.

I have realized, Bear, it does not matter as much if one is really connecting with the animals or not. What really matters is the results obtained, and I have seen some amazing results working with these energies.

Today on the beach I also received intuitive messages to meditate more deeply into the tarot cards using a technique of automatic writing. This was to help get the flow going so that I can open up to receive messages from you. I was thinking the other day, I haven't really felt your communication to guide me like I did the last months when I was at Roy's. I realize you came in when I was very troubled and your guidance comforted me. I haven't been under that stress here.

I enjoy it so much when you speak to me. My intuitive sense is that I need to be more open to you consciously and allow your communication to come through without a dire need on my part. I don't know what it is you will say, but nevertheless it will help me in my understanding of tarot and my connection with you. Then it's not all a one way conversation, now that I know we can communicate. Okay, my dear, I am going to do my tarot meditations and practice some automatic writing. I love you dearly and thank you for being here with me.

Much love,

Your Bee, Loryn

Negative Energies

August 28

Hi, Bear,

I have been home working most of the day and have been using my panther to deal with Agatha. I am amazed at the results. Every time she comes by, I try to remember to bring in the panther. When I do, I feel strong; this has been so helpful. Now all I need to do is continue to use it. I was really not aware of how weak I felt around her.

I remember an experiment I participated in during a Silva Mind Development class with muscle testing. They had me go out of the room not knowing what they would tell the students. When I returned back into the class they tested me and my whole system was weak. It ended up they had all sent negative thoughts at me. It is important that we realize that when we are angry at people we are actually shooting hurtful energy at them and possibly weakening them.

Well, such is life: many people do that. We can't keep ourselves locked up in a closet in order not to feel other's negative energies. We have to find some way to counteract it and now I have found something very useful. I am grateful for my panther. Too bad others can't see my beautiful black cat laying beside me, growling when anyone dares to be any type of threat. She is beautiful and I am grateful for her.

There is another method I have used to protect myself while in the presence of negative energy. I visualize myself in a bubble of golden light, which is fed from the divine source. I ask that this allows positive energy to come in but repels negative energy. Quite often people also unconsciously try to feed off our energy because they haven't yet learned how to connect with their soul. This bubble of light also helps in those circumstances.

I believe working with the animals is more appropriate in this circumstance. Right now my personal energy is not

strong enough to maintain this bubble of light. I need to
work my energy system back up to strength. My situation
with Agatha is a good monitor in terms of where I am with
my energy level.

Enneagram

August 30,

Hello, dear one,

Well, I have some very good news. I told you the other day how using my spirit animal, the panther, was really making me stronger and better able to deal with the situation with Agatha. I know it has been really ridiculous to allow her to get to me, but it has stayed on my mind. Those things that don't leave our mind are there for us to look at until we can be at peace with them.

I finally realized why I have been so on edge around her, especially since she now refuses to talk to me unless absolutely necessary. It is really her own loss because she complains that no one will talk to her. She is receiving the same treatment from others that she is giving me.

She holds everything in. When she does say something to me, it's when she has lost her temper. When she felt the volume of the TV in my room was too loud for her, she screamed at me in a nasty tone of voice to turn it down. The next time she banged on my wall and then screamed at me. Now in my conscious mind I am not afraid of her physically. She is a weak old lady. But it did bring up fear in me that she would burst into my room and explode. I have finally realized that this reaction to her is based on my past experience of when I lived at home with my family. My grandmother, at that time, had a very bad temper and I had extremely sensitive energy. She was not used to dealing with children and was under a lot of stress. Patience with children was not one of her virtues. She had a very dominating personality.

My older brother, Stevan was my best friend for much of my adolescent life. Being children, we would naturally play around and laugh and make noise. I don't ever remember being hit, but I do remember that all my grandmother had to do, was go for the broom as a threat and we would go running. I guess eventually she got her way by controlling us through fear. I remember my grandmother hitting my brother with a shoe and chasing him down the hallway with it. I was so upset that my brother was being hit.

The whole point is when my grandmother was home we were on edge, afraid that if we dare do something wrong in her eyes we would really get it. Eventually my grandmother grew out of this behavior and realized it was not how she wanted to be (my younger brother and sisters never were hit). It did put me in a position of growing up with not much confidence in myself and fear that judgment would end up in physical pain. So here in this present situation I am re-acting from something in the past which has nothing to do with the present. Obviously, I need to get over it. It is an opportunity to gain back some of my power from a very deep, ancient wound. It is helpful for me to have an understanding of why I seem to be acting so irrational. This whole aspect of criticism and judgment is really up for me now. I realized years ago that I also had that aspect of my grandmother in me.

From 1986 -1991, the five years I was involved with Delphi, I did a lot of inner work, mostly through the spiritual psychotherapy process of Ro-Hun, releasing many thought patterns that were most affecting my life in a negative way. I realized that as children we can't help but to pick up the patterns of our parent figures or guardians; but we are not to blame them. I believe we choose the lessons we are to work on while living on earth, Just as we choose the parents (or guardians) to give us the patterns (even the words seem similar) we most need to work through. Then it is up to us to realize what they are, accept them, and then evolve further than they did. Usually it is easy to see what they are because it is usually how we judge them, which means we are judging ourselves. We can't really free ourselves unless we free our judgments of our parent figures.

I understand that, as Wayne Dyer says, "When we judge another we define ourselves." Our need to feel right causes many problems in this world. I had a teacher friend of mine who used to say, just give up the need to be right. We sacrifice love quite often to be right. Look at all the religious wars. We are right and you're wrong, in the name of God; it doesn't make sense. It is helpful first to understand that two people can have their own opinion, and it doesn't mean the other person is wrong. Agatha spends most of her thoughts on how she is right, the way she wants the kitchen, the bathroom, the house. Hers is the right way and everyone else is wrong. It is the only thing she has to cling onto that gives her a sense of confidence. Unfortunately, she has sacrificed the space for love and acceptance of others. She feels lonely and miserable as a result, but at least she is right. She possibly had a similar situation that if she didn't do things the right way, she would be hit or judged in a way that would bring some type of pain.

The Enneagram defines her perfectly and helps me to understand her. She is classified as the Loyalist. When stressed, they become very paranoid, constricted in expression of emotions and eccentric. At their worst they have an authoritative aggressiveness that wants to strike out at others. They end up ruining their desire for security. They become self-defeating persons who are their own worst enemies. If they persist in self-defeating behavior, they will likely drive away everyone on whom they depend. They will be abandoned and alone, the very thing they most fear. Their lesson is to learn to be more secure in themselves, so they do not have to rely on others. Then they do not have to be so angry that others are not giving them what they want, learning to trust themselves so they can be more independent.

The Enneagram is a wonderful and helpful tool for understanding ourselves and others. It also was a turning point in my life in 1983, when I took my first class way before it became popularized. It helped me gain such an understanding of myself and also of my relationships. You were the Peacemaker. You had an extreme amount of patience and were a teacher in that matter for me. I realized years ago that the issues I was dealing with about my grandmother were also issues in myself. First I had to accept I had a strong, angry self hidden within me. Issues of power and control were issues that would continue to come up for me to move through. Real power comes from having that feeling of strength inside, which is what my beautiful black panther helps me with. When we don't feel that power, we have to resort to more dominating behavior. The real power is the power of love and acceptance and that starts with accepting the dark or shadow sides of ourselves, those parts of ourselves that quite often are hiding inside.

For example, I know I have the ability to get very angry. If I judge anger as wrong, which is what I used to do, because I thought spiritual people do not get angry, then I am fighting myself. One day in one of my therapy sessions with a client, I was talking from my heart with a tone of love and acceptance, but it wasn't working. Intuitively I knew I needed to use an angry tone to get through to this particular client, in a way he would hear what I was saying. I thought it was crazy but I did it; he finally started to respond. After the session he told me his mom always talked to him in that tone and that was the tone he associated with love. Even though I wasn't angry with him, I was consciously using the energy of anger in a way that was appropriate at the time. It was an amazing realization for me and it helped to stop judging my anger, and to realize it can be helpful. Now it was a matter of utilizing the energy in a way that was effective, not harmful. Getting angry can be very motivating to move us in a certain direction, one that we want to move in. Where one has to be careful, such as in my childhood, that the anger does not get thrown at someone else in a way that can be harmful to them. Many great leaders become so because of their anger against what seems like injustices in the world, and their desire to do something about it. I do not feel any emotion in us is bad. We are meant, as human beings, to feel all ranges of emotions, but not to allow them to control us. The path is for us to master our emotions. The strength card in the tarot deck, I believe, describes this well as taming the beast within us with love and acceptance.

You were such a great teacher to me in this way. You really disliked arguing and would do your best to avoid it. This was great for me, because it kept me aware of how much it bothered you. I was inspired to find other ways of expression and to create new patterns in myself. My parents bickered a lot and I learned that form of communication for male-female relationships. I seldom argued with women.

You also had experienced the worst of your anger once in a fight and never wanted to reach that point within yourself again; so you had great motivation not to let your anger get the most of you. I do admit I probably was a great test of your patience at times. I can be very persistent. We were good for each other. Our love motivated us to be the best we could be for each other. It motivated us to improve ourselves and work through our own issues.

Well, honey, I have to go for now. I love you much. Loryn

Karma & Past Lives

August 31

Hi Honey,

I keep having intuitive feelings that I am to open myself up to you, so you may communicate with me. I know it was fairly easy to receive your communication when I was in troubled spaces. Those spaces seemed to create an opening for you to come through. We are most apt to receive help when we most need it. Since I know it's possible and it has happened before, I need to find the way to allow it to happen more readily. I guess a lot of things I've been writing about lately have been things I've needed to get out. I thank you for being there, listening and supporting me as I go through my lessons of life.

I saw a movie last night where a guy was doing genetic experiments and another man came along and started criticizing him. The guy's answer, quoted from the bible was, "judge not lest ye be judged," and also "let him who has not sinned cast the first stone." These quotes I had already been thinking of before I saw the movie, and it was amazing for me to hear them come up. Again, it is as if my whole focus right now is in the area of judgment and non-judgment. I remember how many times in my life that I said I would never do something because I had judged it as wrong. I ended up somehow getting involved in exactly what I said I would never do.

It is so easy to judge others. We used to have an American Indian Prayer on our wall that said, "judge not a man until you walk in his moccasins." It is so true. I am beginning to believe we get put in those situations that we once judged as wrong, so that we have a greater understanding and learn not to judge others as being right or wrong. It is not an easy thing to do, but as soon as we learn it, perhaps we will be less apt to experience it again.

I think about it quite often in my art class. In art, there are contests for the best piece of art. One painting could win first prize in one event, and maybe not win a prize at all in another event, because it is all in the eyes of the judges. Art, like many other things that are judged, is a matter of personal opinion. I would think it would be very challenging to be an art teacher. Because everyone has their own personal style, how can one teach that this way is better than that. One would have to be very careful to teach, realizing they are still expressing their own personal viewpoint in certain areas that go beyond the basics of art techniques. I distinctly remember my fourth grade teacher telling me that the way I was coloring was not correct. She showed me another girl's work and told me to do it like hers. But I really liked how I colored my work! We can deeply disrupt someone's freedom to create by telling children the way they are creating is wrong. Being creative is a way we are in alignment with our higher selves. It is how we are born into the likeness of God, the Creator.

So it is with the tarot cards. Many people judge them without knowing anything about them; it shows a lack of knowledge. I understand for some people, the judgment comes from the warning in the Old Testament about avoiding soothsayers, which I can understand. We don't want to put a power into something outside of ourselves, rather than into the power of what we call the Creator, or in our own Higher Self. It is good, though, to have some tools on hand to help give us confirmation of the guidance we receive from our own intuitions. For example, Astrology really got out of control for me when I studied it years ago. I was relating everything to Astrology including the people I met. I wasn't meeting a person but a sign. But now I can use the knowledge of it as a powerful tool for understanding things in my life. It is pretty common knowledge that the moon affects us as human beings. Ask any police department, bartender, or hospital, how many things pick up around the time of the full moon. We cannot deny there are planetary influences. If the moon affects the huge bodies of ocean waters what makes us think our own bodies, which are mostly water, are not affected. Some knowledge of those influences can be beneficial at certain times in our life.

I have realized more and more how we need to have faith, but our faith needs to rest upon personal experiences also, not just blind faith. We need to realize also that a good amount of material that is spread around as truth, are beliefs, not knowings. We all rely on beliefs until we gain our own knowings through personal experience. We just need to remain aware of that as we live our lives. We need to test the information we receive.

I am amazed myself at the things I once thought were truths and now have realized they are not. I know they can serve a purpose to believe in temporarily.

Like the idea of hell. Being raised a Catholic, I was told if, we as Catholics committed a mortal sin, (breaking one of the Ten Commandments), and died without going to confession, we would burn in hell for eternity. I was terrified because one of the Ten Commandments was to obey your parents. Well, like any child, I was never totally obedient. After grammar school I started to question what I had been taught. I remember in first grade the first thing we learned about God was, God is love, and all forgiving. So how could an all-forgiving God punish me in hell for happening to die at a time when I didn't get a chance to confess? It didn't make sense to me. As I started studying mysticism and other religions, I started to believe more in different levels in the afterlife. Truly if one lived a sinful, hateful life, void of love, then they would also continue that type of life in the afterworld. It would be very reflective of the kind of life they already had on earth. I believe the concept of hell is a helpful one. I do not try to convince those that strongly believe it as part of their religious beliefs to think otherwise. There are many people who need the fear of going to hell to keep their values in alignment. For years, the fear of hell has kept people on good behavior. But I am at a place in my life where I do not need fear to keep me in line. I am aware of karma, and what ye sow ye shall reap. So, "do unto thy neighbors as you would have them do unto you". I seem to be doing a lot of Bible quoting here, honey, but it's what comes up, so I write it down.

I also believe in some form of, what people call reincarnation. I do know that we live in a dimension that experiences time, so I believe on some level we can have different experiences on earth. Since there really is no time in your dimension, the way of describing coming back is just a way that is easy for our minds to understand it. I did a lot of past life regressions both on myself and as therapy on others. I have seen over and over the benefits people receive from tapping into their subconscious and bringing up memories from what seems like other existence's. Using the information gives them insight into their present life. I am not out to prove its existence. As I said before, I prefer to share what I know from personal experience rather than what the books say, or even the experts say. That is what I know is a truth. I have learned much about myself from the many, what we call, past lives I have seen myself in. There were certain patterns I saw myself repeating over and over again which motivated me to change. There were talents I saw I had like dancing that motivated me to continue to move in that direction. Seeing my past lives helped me to understand some of my fears and made it easier to release them.

One other thing I realized by seeing my past lives is how deeply rooted our beliefs are in the thought, "When we do good we are rewarded, and if we do bad we are punished." There is some truth to that if we believe, "What ye sow, ye shall reap." The problem is I have seen people not take charge in their lives, because they feel God must be punishing them for something they have done wrong. That is where we also need to understand there are other truths that come into play. It would not have been very beneficial for me to believe that when you died, God must be punishing me for something I did in the past. I don't know how I would have gotten over it. Instead, to realize and know that the Creator is an all loving being and if anything happens like that to me, there must be a higher reason that I do not yet know. Looking back I can see tremendous things I have learned and ways in which I have grown as a result of your death. Since you are not really dead, just your body is gone, and you are still here in spirit form, your death can be considered a gift.

That is again where the Tarot cards come in. They show people seemingly bad situations are really meant to be situations one can receive value from, rather than feeling like a victim. In the Tarot, the Death cards means transformation, because nothing in life dies, only changes form. Water may seem to disappear when it evaporates, yet really it just changes form and becomes moisture in the air. There is always a higher perspective people can take to get them through difficult times.

I remember when we decided to do a past life regression on you to understand why you had this obsession with fishing. You wanted to change your career to be a fisherman. It showed a successful life as a fisherman in a village in Norway. There were many challenges involved, sometimes having to stay out at sea for weeks at a time. In a short summary you realized that being a fisherman was attached to a feeling of notoriety and success. Those good feelings attached to fishing were why you enjoyed it so much. Afterward, you realized you were not willing to stay out at sea for weeks at a time, and gave up on the idea.

So was it really a past life? I don't know for sure. Even if we could check the guys name out, and the village, it still doesn't mean he was you. You still could have tapped into a similar pattern to gain greater understanding. What I do know is the information helped you to relax a bit about fishing and to have a greater understanding about yourself.

I have heard that Christians at one time had reincarnation as their belief system until someone decided they were going to change it. It certainly appears so in the Bible when someone asked Jesus, "Why was this man born blind? Was it something he did or his parents?" Or when asked if he was Elijah come back. These questions certainly imply this belief.

I guess I went off the topic of Tarot, which is what I was writing about. Studying and using the cards have been giving me such an understanding of the working of life and the paths that we all, as human beings, go through. With all the different combinations I can still see that we are really all learning the same things. We think our situation is unique. In one way it is, but in another way we all have the same lessons, just in different combinations.

A New Level

Hi, Bear,

A lot has been going on that I have to catch up with. I am back at my sisters'. We had a psychic fair here recently over the Labor Day weekend and I went to check it out. I ended up getting a reading from a woman who usually is very expensive with a reputation of being very good. I figured it would be fun just to see and learn her method of Tarot readings. I was not that familiar with the cards that she used. I've seen them before, but they are ones that I don't particularly feel a connection to for my own personal use. Anyway, she kept asking me if I was married or in a relationship. I said no, and she seemed quite perplexed.

I saw her looking at my ring that I wear on my left ring finger, which one could easily assume is a wedding ring. I remember when we were sitting down counting all the change in your piggy bank with your friend. You wouldn't tell me why. Then two days later you gave me the most beautiful, dainty, heart shaped, gold ring with a diamond in the center. I absolutely loved it, although I am not usually one to wear much jewelry. I tend to want to take it off. You said it was a temporary ring for me to wear until you could afford to get me an engagement ring. You said you wanted the men out there to know I was already taken. It took me a while getting used to wearing it. I used to take it off as soon as I got home because it just seemed to get in the way. Sometimes you would feel hurt if I forgot to wear it to work. So I wore it for you at first, and then I got used to it. Now I wear it almost all the time. I know some people, like the Tarot reader, assume I am married but that is okay. I would prefer right now that men not approach me and in a way, I still feel quite married to you. I finally told the reader this to relieve her confusion. I told her I had lost you a year ago to death and I still felt married to you. I could understand why the cards would read about my relationship to you, because I am so much in communication with you.

After hearing that she took my hands and asked me what your name was. I could tell she was going to try to psychically contact you. The first thing she asked me was if you had heart problems and I said, "yes." She asked if you had died of a heart attack, because she saw you showing her your heart. That was a good confirmation to know that indeed she had made contact with you. I could feel the intense energy of love when she made the contact. She told me you supported me in moving on with my life. She said you were concerned about me not eating enough food. I laughed at that because compared to how much you ate, I do eat very little. You weighed 100 pounds more than me. She told me how you mentioned spending time with the dog, and also how you were involved in a new project of sending hope to the planet.

I asked her to ask you about our communication. She said that you were suggesting breathing techniques to assist me in allowing you to come through for me in the writing. I explained I was already familiar with that. It was just that I had been feeling I needed to allow you to come through, but I didn't know what to ask you, or what my intention should be. This had always been my problem with the spirit world. I have been trained quite often in connecting to higher mind, inner guides and teachers. I have been able to do it with great ease. When I had personal problems I could receive guidance. But what to do to keep up the communication was where I was unsure. It is like that in art classes. Though many of the women were great painters, they say their problem was running out of ideas to paint.

She also said you have a group of friends that would like to communicate about your project, and things that deal with the people of the earth on a world wide scale. Like the hope that the people of the earth need right now and the things you all are doing to provide that hope. She said you would be the one who would sort of regulate who came through, and I could even ask for assistance to formulate the best questions to ask.

I was excited about this new project for us and I went home and began writing right away, but I did it on a note pad. I am going to rewrite here what I wrote, hopefully being able to understand my own handwriting.

My beloved Bear,

Please tell me what you're involved with that is helpful
for me to know.

(Hope to the Planet)

My beloved Bee,

So wonderful to connect with you again; you are so beautiful, such a glowing star. Your beauty outshines the beauty of the most beautiful sunset. I am here with you dear, always, and am very excited about our communication. On earth I knew your beauty, but from here your inner sensitivity and beauty outshines what I knew you to be.

Dear one, I will tell you now what I am beginning to do with my friends here. Our project is to assist the planet to raise its vibrations. Raising its vibration is a must and part of the Divine Plan. It is time to bring the deeper and the darker into the light to expand it. We are sending light rays to the planet with new messages of hope that will hopefully seep through into the people's minds and thoughts. You see how certain mind and thought influences can help the planet; for example, how the idea of angels have now so influenced the earth.

The World Reflects Our Thoughts

September 9

Dear Bear,

Hello, Beloved. How grateful I am to have you in my life, although I must say these past few days I have gotten tearful quite often when seeing someone that looks like you or other matters that remind me of you. I do miss you here with me on the planet. I hope you forgive me for my tears. I miss being able to lay in your arms, feel your body next to mine and feel your loving arms around me, protecting me from the world that at times can seem so harsh.

I have come to a great realization about myself recently that has come about from many so called hints from the universe. I recently spoke with Roy on the phone and he shared a frustration he had with me during our relationship. He had felt I would not open up to him. After that conversation, I picked a card from the Joy of Relationship card deck. I asked what I most needed to learn. The card came up suggesting barriers. This fit in right along with what he had said. I thought about it and saw that indeed I did stop opening up to him. I didn't feel it was safe to do so. I had a fear of being hurt.

I took a healing bath the other night with a special combination of oils that were intuitively picked for me. I asked what I needed at the moment. I realized that I had deep fears that the world was not a safe place and this related back to the topic concerning judgment. If I believe the world is not a safe place, then I will attract situations which would reflect back to me what I believe. Even with you and me, I opened my heart more so than I ever had in my life. I got hurt, and after you left, felt even more that the world was not a safe place. It was a place with a lot of harshness and cruelty. I know I didn't believe this totally, because I also know the world is many other things and that the universe provides all I need.

I was amazed to see how this thought pattern has been

working out in my life for so long. During the healing bath, I worked on changing this thought pattern. I looked to see what I could choose to believe to replace the belief of not being or feeling safe. The one that came up for me was that I am truly a spirit, and my physical body is only a temporary vehicle for my spirit. My spirit cannot be hurt physically. So, my true nature was beyond being hurt in any way. *(baby steps)*

My dear Bee,

I hold you in my arms of love as you move through your sadness. I have been with you, and may it be a comfort for you to know that, Beloved One, I understand. It is much to expect those still on the planet to live in such an awareness as you have stated - to be able to rise above, or be willing to rise above and accept one's place in the responsibility of the happenings of life. The ego is very resistant to it. One must live in constant vigilance of what is happening in one's life. The sadness, dear one, as you know is part of the human experience. Allow yourself to feel deeply and move in the direction of joy. Allow these situations to remind you to devote yourself to finding your true Self through joy. When you have more and more experiences of joy in your life, you know you are more connected to your Higher Self that is always radiating that joy. The human experience is an amazing thing with many complexities to it. The amount of potential growth that humans go through for their evolution is tremendous. I know it does not seem so when we are living on the earth, but when you look at it from this viewpoint there is so much cause for applause.

Think of the challenges a child has when learning its first steps. It is inspired inward to begin to walk, it falls constantly and it's even painful at times. The level of accomplishment, once it walks on its own, is tremendous.

Remember Bee, the baby steps. I am glad I had you watch that movie (What about Bob?). Sweet, sweet Bee, I surround you with my love. Allow the sadness to be there. Acknowledge it as an honor to the love that we shared. Thank yourself for being willing to go into the depths and feel it. Acknowledge it as part of your human experience. Thank it for reminding you of your feelings and love it. Then allow yourself to move on toward the next step in your life, being grateful for all the things you have learned. You are not alone. My love for you is here constantly. Dear one, take some time now to allow us to connect and be together in the energy of love that we know so well together.

Thank you, Bear, I will now.

Part Four

Letters from the Jersey Shore

Sacred Trance Dance

September 28

Hi, my Bear, my sweet, sweet love,

It has been such a long time since I last wrote, at least it seems that way. I really love writing to you, even though you already know much of what I write. I realize it helps me to be able to write to you. It adds a level of physicality to the experience of communicating to you. When I re-read the communication from you; I feel love and am amazed and deeply touched by your words and your support. I have always deeply respected you and am honored to still be a part of your life. Thank you. Your death has affected my life so greatly. I continue to pull out more and more value from the experience of continuing to live through your death, and to share with others what I am learning.

I drove from Florida to New Jersey and am now at Brenda's home. She is my youngest sister. She has a small apartment in South Jersey near a busy intersection about fifteen minutes from the beach. My god-daughter Stephanie lives an hour north with her family and my dad lives a half-hour south.

I just returned from Omega Institute in New York after teaching my first Trance Dance Presenters Class. It was wonderful. I feel grateful for the experience. I love dancing so much, as you well know. I am excited about Trance Dance for myself personally. I just place my intention, do some deep breathing to alter my consciousness, put on a blindfold, put the music on, surrender to spirit, let go and dance into bliss. It is such a quick and joyful way to move through my own processes. My natural way is to share with others what has worked so well for me. I love to teach and have always wanted to be a teacher since I was in the first grade. I have usually found a way to teach; such as, yoga, fitness, meditation, healing, mind development, Montessori pre-school, art, art education, and most recently Trance Dance and training others to present Trance Dance. I have always had this inner need to do this. I am happier in my life when I have this outlet. I believe the universe gives messages that guide us in the best direction on our path . I realized this more when I saw that past life as an American Indian going on a vision quest. In that life, the message to the boy from the Great Spirit was to fulfill his purpose by working with the horses. This was his great love. All along his love for and his ability to work with them was his soul guiding him on his path. I know my path is about finding my own way through life's challenges by following my inner guidance and then sharing with others what I have learned, knowing my first responsibility is to my own relationship with my Higher Self/God.

Trance Dance is where I am right now. It was good to dance again especially after all my tests and challenges with Agatha. Of course I didn't let go as much as I usually do because I have to keep in touch with the class, but there were a few times I was able to let go and have my own experiences. The one clear message I received is that I was being given the free time now, right now, to write.

I came back from Omega with a much more focused attitude on continuing my writings with you. I realize how important it is for me to do this now, because later I may not have the time. My sense is something will come up where my life will get very busy again. What has been so great is that I have been able to use a computer where ever I go. I had one at Mari's, and now at Brenda's I have access to two computers. One at her local library and one at her school. Spirit really has provided me with what I need.

Teaching at Omega has enabled me to return to my birth sate, New Jersey, to visit family and friends and to continue to write. And maybe later check out teaching yoga again.

The afternoon that I was able to dance with the class at Omega felt very good. I felt my body again; it was such a sigh of relief and feeling of gratitude. I was also grateful to be in a place where I could have the exhilarating music loud enough where I could feel the vibrations penetrate my body. I could really let go and come home to myself. I felt the joy of being in the body and being connected to the spirit at the same time. Every time I go into that space I feel such gratitude for the experience. Every day I kept feeling more and more alive, even though that afternoon was the only time I went deep into the dance. The other times, while the class was dancing, I would stay in a light trance so I could keep in touch with the class and still dance. Its good practice for me to go into trance with my eyes open and it gets easier and easier. Even my sister commented on how much better I looked after I came back from Omega.

It was even greater for the participants. I could see how they were all getting brighter and brighter. I just loved seeing the students go through numerous spiritual experiences throughout the week. They were having many realizations about themselves that allowed them to help heal their personal problems. And the other great thing about Trance Dance, unlike a therapy session, is you don't have to rely on someone else to do it for you.

Ultimately we are to learn from our own inner voice. The advantage of a group experience with Trance Dance is the group sharing done at the end. It gives one the opportunity to get clarification and confirmation on ones own experience. Once we do it enough, it gets easier to do it on our own, although it's good at times to have support from our fellow human beings. This is especially true when unexpected, strong, emotional responses come up with certain realizations. There have been times when the dance has brought up grieving for people. I know from experience, it is comforting to know someone else is there who cares, as we go through our own processes. I am so excited about Trance Dance. I have seen it heal relationship issues, guide people on their true path and so much more.

The first for me is the joy I have dancing. It puts a smile on my face. Then it combines the physical, mental and the spiritual. We all need to live a balanced life. It is a form of physical exercise, mentally it both frees and focuses the mind, and spiritually it brings in the breath and the three work as one.

Furthermore, I use Trance Dance to release stressful emotions. When I feel frustrated or angry, the dance helps to release negative energy. Then I feel lighter and freer. At the same time my mind is open to receive intuitive messages that guide me in handling the situation.

For example, I was feeling uneasy about knowing what direction I was going into next. While dancing I received a message that I was right where I was supposed to be in my life and I need to keep focusing on my writing with you.

This amazing dance has been able to heal kinks in my body quicker than any other method. One time, for some reason, my spine felt out of alignment and as I Trance Danced I felt everything move back into its proper place.

Trance Dance has awakened an aliveness in my body and in many others beyond what has been felt before. The life force energy flows through one's body as one moves into a state of ecstasy. A passion for life awakens to be used wherever it is needed. Some use it in their work, in their sexual relationships, and/or in their creativity.

With Trance Dance I feel my power. I am still calling it forth and am becoming increasingly energized. Now I can dance and go into spontaneous energizing experiences that absolutely empower and balance me. These experiences connect me with a profound spiritual energy very quickly.

I have received many visions in Trance Dance where I realized greater truths of the world. For example, when we move into these states of consciousness we are assisting in healing the planet. By raising our energy vibrations we are spinning off the lower sticky vibrations. It's like taking a shower, or even swimming in the ocean and then walking in the sun. Afterwards one feels so much cleaner, lighter, and freer.

A vision I had during Trance Dance at the Natale Institute, in the Netherlands, was a connection with other Trance Dancers all over the world. I felt as if I were connected to Trance Dancers in the present, past, and future all in the same moment. It was as if we were all one tribe and I had reconnected with them. When we danced we were all connected on an energetic level, and were somehow connected with the energy of the planet. I know quite often when I am presenting a Trance Dance class I can sense groups of other spirit beings on the planet dancing with us. Of course, Bear, you always show up. I just love when you pop in and begin to dance with me. You always put a smile on my face. I feel joy in my heart when we are able to spend time dancing.

I received confirmation on this when I was presenting a Trance Dance class in Atlanta. While we were sharing our experiences during the dance, a woman asked what happened to the man who had come in late during the class. She said she had stepped out of the room temporarily and when she returned she saw a man who hadn't been there in the beginning of the class. She assumed he had come in late. When I asked her to describe him, she described you perfectly. I had already experienced you in the class as I normally do. Every class, at some time, you usually pop in unexpectedly and dance with me.

I have used the dance to focus my energies for healing from a distance. I had a friend who had recently been in the hospital for surgery and I went into trance while dancing. I had my tambourine out; I visualized him in my mind and sent healing energy of light and love to support him through his healing process.

I love using it for manifesting. Trance Dance really allows me to gain a strong focus of attention. I visualize what I want to create in my life. I usually now focus more on the feelings I wish to have, rather than the actual material objects. I just send energy to these pictures. I can feel these energies are powerfully focused. I love doing full moon and new moon dancing rituals for manifesting.

Power animals quite often come up in dancing. Mine come in occasionally. I have had many people, even those who haven't ever studied Shamanism, have experiences with animals and their powers during the dance.

I have had just a few small glimpses into what seemed like past life memories during different types of music. There are others though that have had very full, deep, past life memories come up for them.

One very powerful part of the dance for me, Bear, is being able to express myself. Somehow, moving my body however it wants, allows me to be who I am. There is a part of us all that have, what I call, a wild self. Our society does not necessarily have acceptable ways for us to express that wild self. We are told we need to stay in control of ourselves at all times and repress our energies. Our sexuality is one way that people express that part of themselves. Although, even sexually, some people feel they can not totally let go lest they be judged. I love my wild self. I love to feel her. I love to let her dance. I love to feel her energy. I love her power. I love the freedom I feel when she dances through me.

When I was at Omega we had an open evening where everyone was invited to come in to Trance Dance. I know you were there and enjoying the energy as much as I. There were about eighty to one hundred people. Many of those people were the younger group that was on staff. I could feel them allowing their wild selves out to dance and feel the freedom they were feeling inside. They were taking the opportunity to express this part of themselves. It was so wonderful; the energy was so intense. When we were all finished, I felt the greater sense of peace they had inside of them as a result of expressing their wildness.

Surprisingly, a man came into the class that I never would have expected to be there. He didn't seem the type to want to experience the dance, perhaps because he appeared to be the conservative type. After the dance he shared with me a wonderful story that explained to me why he was there. He had recently gotten sick, and was up at Omega to work through some of his health issues. A few weeks before, while he was receiving a healing session, a big African man appeared to him in his mind and told him he needed to dance to get better. That was why he came to the class. While he was dancing, the African man came and danced through him; they were together in spirit. He was able to let go and move in ways he had never moved before. He said he really enjoyed dancing because he felt so wonderful and joyous. He could now understand why the dancing could help him get healthier.

Trance Dance is a wonderful form of meditation for me. I enjoy meditating and being still, but it is also great to meditate and be active. I still receive all the benefits of being in the meditative state while dancing. Going into these altered states of mind helps me to release stress and regenerate more quickly. It allows me to free the mind and allow spiritual guidance to come forth. I feel more energized. I love taking the time to be with my soul.

I had a wonderful experience in Greece, Trance Dancing with my soul. I had already done four months of pretty intense healing work on myself in Europe, which included five days of soul hunting during the previous month. After the soul hunting experience, I felt so much stronger when I returned to the United States. In fact, my whole outside world changed very quickly, which I know was a reflection of how my inner world changed. The soul hunting experience was very powerful. I loved how on all my soul hunts you showed up with my power animals, an old American Indian man and a beautiful American Indian woman dressed in white with long black hair. We all met and went on a journey, looking for the parts of myself I needed to bring back with me.

By the time I got to Greece, I was already in a much better space. During the Trance Dance there I experienced another level of soul hunting. Instead of bringing back some of the parts that had left from past traumas, I started to gather parts of my soul that were light, free and joyful. I moved into this wonderful place of bliss where I saw myself in a swirl of bright golden light. I felt I was one with a whole group of beautiful light beings, and yet I could still feel my own individuality. I was dancing in a swirl and the whole swirl was my soul. I kept getting a sense I was dancing with all of my essence. It was an expanding, ecstatic experience.

I have also had experiences during the dance where I felt a deep connection to the earth. I felt so much love for her. I could really feel how my body and hers were connected in some way. It was also a very sensual experience. I sensed the importance of keeping an earth awareness.

Another fun part of Trance Dance, which is really what I enjoy about any type of social dancing, is that there is a real feeling of community between those that are dancing together. I believe that was why it was part of ancient cultures to dance together, so the group could feel as one unit. Some of the highlights of my life have been at family weddings and I was on the dance floor with all of my family. I do have this thing where I love to be dancing with the ones I love. I think that is something the modern American culture lacks, the times where community come together to dance in celebration as one.

There are, of course, all types of music to dance to. As you know, I was looking for a type of music that would really move me to dance. I have now been opened to much more music over the past year. My favorite is Natale's *Shaman's Breath*, made specifically for Trance Dance. The bookstore at Omega sold out after I played it on the opening evening. So I guess others felt the same. It puts me in a deep space for Trance Dance experiences. There are other types of music I still enjoy dancing to and different cultural music elicits different things within me. I love dancing to American Indian music, Latin music, Middle Eastern music and Hawaiian music.

Well, Bear, as you can tell being involved with Trance Dance has been good for me. It has been one of those joys added to my life that has helped me in replacing the joy of sharing life with you. I am finding more and more ways to be joyful and not to rely on something outside of myself. I have been reaching deeper within myself to experience a true joy that can not be taken away. In this way, I feel I am much more connected to the true source of joy; the Source of all there is, what some call God or the Universal Energy. I am much more apt to be able to live more abundantly. I believe the sadness of your loss will always be with me, and it is not something I have to try to get rid of or avoid. It is something I can live with, accept, and continue to live on, seeking the fulfillment that only living my true self can give me.

I am grateful that the experience of your death led me to this realization of what I need to do to live life more fully. I hope to honor you by realizing and fulfilling what lessons I have been taught and am still learning. I thank you for what you have given me through your own death on this planet. It has truly been a gift toward greater understanding of my true self. I pray that I may honor you by realizing all I have been given through you.

I have to go now, Bear; I love you much and thanks for listening.

Prayers for the Departed

October 1

Dear Bear,

Yesterday Brenda and I went into New York to visit the Museum of Modern Art. As we walked up Fifth Avenue from Penn Station, we came upon St. Patrick's Cathedral. We went in to look around and a Mass was just starting. It was the most sacred part of the Mass, when the priest was representing Jesus at the Last Supper, blessing the bread and wine. I know you were never really one to go to church. I suggested it every once in a while just for the experience. You grew up as a Seventh Day Adventist and I was curious what their mass was like. Many people pull away from the church when they have unpleasant memories associated around it, as you did.

I was raised a Catholic and have found the teachings of Jesus Christ and the Blessed Mother very helpful in my life. Half my family was Jewish and I studied Hinduism during my yoga trainings. I have spent time here and there in Unity Churches, studied Shamanism, Huna and other philosophies. Through this I have been able to find value in all teachings. I was amazed to find all the similarities, and to find what the differences were that seem to separate people.

Anyway, during the Mass I was paying close attention when the priest was having us pray for those that have departed. I realized how all along the Catholics, if not all Christians, have a strong belief in the afterlife. I know at funerals it was emphasized to send prayers for those that have departed. And I know in other religions there is also much emphasis on the afterlife.

I remember after you died, a female acquaintance of mine called me to share with me a Buddhist ritual around death. She suggested I go back to your place of death to say a prayer because quite often souls need help departing from that spot. I appreciated her wanting to help, but I knew we had done enough meditations into the spirit world that for sure you knew your way there. Before I left Hawaii, I did return to your place of death, and it brought tears to my eyes again. I wonder what it must be like for the Miller's to have that spot in the back of their house as a constant memory of your death. They did also love you, as you and your father had been a part of their life for years.

I realized also, in church, that it is always good to pray for the departed, no matter what. Prayer is good for everything. Everyone could always use some extra light. Plus, the experience of praying for you is good for me, as it gives me another time of feeling very connected to you. So I lit a candle for you and prayed that you be filled with light. I felt you as I prayed and tears once again came to my eyes. I am not sure what the tears are about anymore. It just seemed part of an expression of my deep feelings associated with you and my life. Once I try to put a label on the reason, it seems to dilute it in some way.

I used to think when I didn't respond with tears anymore, it meant I was healed. Now I believe that my acceptance of the tears and my depth of feelings is the greatest part of my healing. I know having to live through the experience of your death and finding my way back to joy is part of my path of remembering who I really am, a beautiful spiritual being having a human experience. Your death has anchored me so much more into my spiritual being. I dove in so much deeper in order to gain the energy to pull me through.

Honey, I feel like you would like to come through now and speak to me, so I will shift my mode and listen.

(Divine Connection)

My dear Bee,

So good to connect with you again. I would love it if you took time each day to continue to connect with me at this deep level like you were doing for a while. I do enjoy it so much and it is of great benefit to us both as it gives the conscious feeling of being connected to the great Divine, just as we did on a daily basis when I was still with you in the physical.

Beloved Bee, you're such sweet nectar. Such bliss I feel when we connect. It is as if I am laying in a field of fragrant flowers on a warm, sunny day in a big open field of grass. My Bee, I am in awe and in wonder with you. You're such a beautiful spirit and soul. I am grateful that we can spend this time connecting in this way until you arrive here to be with me in spirit. Your work is a very important part of your growth. I can see you completing something you have been working on for a long time. This time for you on the planet, is what could be called a pivotal point. You have done well in getting through this transitional time period in your life. It has been difficult for me also to have the experience of watching you go through your periods of sadness. You know I never ever liked it when you cried. It has never been easy for me to know you were sad. So I also had to go through my lessons here in trusting the Divine in what was happening for you in your life was what was best. At first I was not able to see in what direction you were headed. Perhaps it was because you had not clearly chosen yourself. But as you became clearer and clearer I could see the wonderful direction you're heading in your life. I can marvel at the magnificence of the divine plan. I can see now that perhaps yours is the greatest challenge in being the one who stays behind. Your pattern is the one that is disrupted. Whereas, the

one who leaves has the distraction of all the new pat-
terns that are to be created. I mostly have a sense of
peace throughout this all as I am directed to follow my
own path here, knowing that you're okay now. There
have been times where that peace has been tested while
watching you lose your own sense of peace.

Right now I do have the space to watch over you
and work with you as we have been doing. I am grate-
ful for that. I also have another project that I have that
I can do simultaneously as I work with you. As I have
mentioned before, we are working on the effect of color
frequencies. I know since I shared this with you before
you have been taking more notice on the effect of color.

(effects of color)

Yes, honey that is for sure. When I was visiting a health
center last week there was so little color in the room. The
rug was a grayish blue and the blanket a similar color. It
seemed so dreary. There was nothing on the walls and they
were a dull white. I immediately hung up all my turquoise
and teal clothes, which is normally my favorite color to wear,
although I have been wearing a lot of black lately. I also

hung up your silk shirt that I carry around, the one you were wearing when I met you. Hanging up all of my clothes on the wall gave the room color, which made it feel so much better. Our world here would be so dreary if everything was without color. I know I could go on and on about all the ways color affects me and others. I also took notice as to how the colors on the trees were beginning to change from green to such beautiful hues of gold, orange, red and yellow. Although I don't particularly prefer the colder weather, compared to Florida or Hawaii, I did enjoy being able to see the change of the fall colors.

So what more are you doing with colors?

We are experimenting with different hues of colors and their affect on the people on the planet. We are inspiring people to try out different colors in different places. Already much work has been done on the planet in this area in many public areas. It is a very subtle, yet powerful way to make changes. For example, if you tell hospital personnel how important and helpful it would be for them to spend more time in their heart and how much more it would benefit the healing of the patients, their minds could come up with many excuses of why they can't or don't. But if you put a soft pink color around, like painting the wall pink, this would have a softening effect on the heart naturally, for some people. On a subtle level they would be inclined to be more caring. The experimental part is that different colors can have different affects on people. Some people enjoy the gray skies on a cloudy day and some people feel depressed. So it is finding hues of color that have the most effect on the greatest amount of people and then getting those colors implemented.

Honey, I am very surprised by this because I would have expected you to be doing some different type of work. Like I have sensed you at different times working and creating art with wood. Also, when we contacted you from Delphi you were working with sound. This color work is not anything I saw you involved with much while you were here on earth. Why the switch?

Well Bee, in one way the sound and color work very closely together because we are working with frequen-

cies. I was working with wood, music and making projects just as taking some time to play and create and I still do. I do many different things while here. I create, I watch over and work with you, I take classes in living on earth, I have spiritual studies. It's different than earth in the sense I am able to do more things in a variety of different ways. In your terms you might call it multidimensional, doing things on different levels at once. We are multidimensional beings on earth. We just don't realize it as much because of the limited thought patterns we choose to believe. Working with colors is a lot of fun. There are a group of beings that I am connected with that are involved in the project to benefit earth. I was suggesting to you, Bee, to take that art class. I wanted you to see the powerful effects of color.

You little sneak. I did love that class. The first day all I did was play with the different colors and all the different shades of color I could make. It was so therapeutic for me in so many different ways. But Bear, I still don't get exactly what you're doing.

It's similar to your Trance Dance work. You're aware that the dancing alters your vibration to a place that feels better. Once you feel better everything in your life goes better. In the healing work you did, you worked on changing the vibration to get more aligned with the divine order of things. That allowed other natural healing processes to take place. When we did hands on healing together, our intention was to bring through the divine light of love into the other person's energy field. Then healing could take place on whatever level was best. The colors do the same.

I am getting a sense of what you're saying, honey. I guess my way of doing things is to gear toward things that are deep and intensely transforming. Like in Trance Dance, one notices effects right away. But the color works on such a subtle level. I have been paying more and more attention to the power that color has in my life.

When I was doing the art regularly, the color was so much a part of the effect of the piece. I am very choosy about colors and probably always have been. One thing that caught my attention was when I was saving this on the computer another color came onto the screen to emphasize a point. It was a bright pink color. Very pretty and emphasized by the beautiful blue color of the screen which was the shade of blue you most loved. In fact even now as I write this I am noticing more the effect of how I am enjoying this blue screen. The words on the bottom are in light blue and the words on the screen a light yellow with a tinge of green. Working with colors while being on the computer certainly make it a more enjoyable experience than working with black and white all the time. But what caught my attention was this bright pink color which has been sort of a new shade of color that I have seen more and more in clothes. I know it is a heart color and can sense what an effect it would have if it were around more often.

I also sense though, as in my art, it is not about just one color, which is what I thought when you first told me about this, but it is also about how one color intermixes with another color. One thing that makes this pink so pretty is how it has the blue surrounding it.

Yes, Bee, you're correct in your sensing. It is part of the play on the planet. One color intermixing with another. One energy intermixing with another. Like the male, female; yin, yang; and joy, sadness. You learn about one by going to the extreme of the opposite. As for you, the depth of our joy was what put you into the depth of your sadness. You have a greater appreciation for joy. You have been so deep into the darkness where your joy was hidden from you. It wasn't that it was not there; it was just that you were choosing to experience another aspect of the same energy. Part of the human experience is to experience all aspects of human life to gain experiences for the soul. That is, to experience both the darkness and the light and then moving into a space where you rise above the duality of it all, back up into a space where all is one. But all aspects of self must be experienced and accepted.

I had a difficult time understanding this while I was on the planet. How could the bad also be the good? Yet another part of me also knew that God was all good. I had experienced in our meditations the oneness of all *things. Yet as we rose up in meditations I could see that there really was no bad. It was just myself and others having human experiences and learning our way. What seemed to be mistakes were feedback on what didn't work and what needed to be readjusted.*

Honey, I have to take a break now. It has been wonderful writing so much with you, but it has taken a lot to focus my attention so long on bringing you in. I will continue again tomorrow, and I promise I will be paying more attention to the effect of colors now with much more conscious awareness. I love you dearly and once again am deeply appreciative that we can have this connection.

Much love to you, dear one.

Seeing All That You Have

October 2

Hello my beloved,

Yesterday was quite an experience for me, focusing so long and deep on what you wanted to communicate to me. I could feel a difference on the affect on my energy. It was similar to the feeling I had the first time I did the Tarot readings for five hours straight. I am ready today to go further into this space with you and am excited to hear more of what you have to say. I feel our communication went very well yesterday.

So, tell me more Bear about what you're doing.

Hello my darling Bee,

Thank you for connecting with me and our love again. Such a pleasure to connect with you and to work together with you like this. I love you, little one, and am grateful for our relationship. Never had I ever expected a relationship to turn out like this. It has definitely been a healing from all past relationships for me to know and experience the value of a love on such a deep level that has its association through God and the Divine. I know you still feel deeply that you wish I was there with you. As we continue on, my beautiful one, you will continue to see more and more of the value of us being like this. How amazing it is, dear one, for two beings that are associated with the earth plane to relate like this. If you remember, from the very beginning, we saw through the tarot cards that our relationship was to be an example to others - the pattern of a good relationship. It is important to take time together to connect with the love and the connection with the Divine. It is also important to experience gratitude on a daily basis for the beloved ones that we have in our lives. Hopefully, people realize it is a gift to be able to touch their loved ones physically, to feel the beauty of the skin, to smell the scents of the body, to hear the sound of the beloved's voice, and being able to physically see them there. These things are to be fully appreciated while we have that time together on earth. Hopefully, others will take the time to have the realization of what it would be like if all of a sudden that person they slept next to was not there anymore, to realize all the little things that couples tend to bicker about are such a waste of time. For us, I know money was a great challenge. We needed not to get stressed out about how much money we had and letting those thoughts overpower the appreciation for what we did have. I know we did spend time with this awareness. I remember a week before our wedding I asked you about how important our love was and was it the most important thing in life, even greater than our money issues. You smiled and said yes, honey. Our love is the most important thing. We did have to keep reminding ourselves how much time is wasted worrying about what one doesn't have, rather than realizing the greatness of all the abundance that is on the planet.

Tell me more about the work you're doing, honey. Is there something you would like to share with me about what you have learned about color?

(good vibrations)

Bee, there is so much and I am really quite amazed that I had such little realization of it while I was on earth. I did appreciate the beauty of nature while living in Hawaii. The colors were so fabulous and incredible. We just loved the colors of the rainbows and the sunsets. I just never stepped back to witness what an affect these colors had on my life. The color of the ocean was also something I loved and was part of the reason we loved being out there. Quite often we were just surrounded with blues. You notice now with your art class how many colors may be out there in the sky. We think of it as just blue, but when we observe more closely, there are incredible amounts of different shades of blue. Part of the reason why nature is so healing is because of the vibration of the colors that are so vibrant. Even sound has a color to it. It is the vibrations that we are

Last night honey I did a meditation and I had this sense about colors and vibrations. I want to head in the direction of a finer, lighter, vibration of peace. I sensed what it would be like living in that vibration of just light. I have touched those spaces of being completely one with the light. There is a sense of total bliss and beauty. It was like one color, one light, one experience. And I can see how after living on the planet, we would yearn to live in this space of peace.

But then, I had this realization of how great it is to live in the diversity of all the experiences here. It is sort of like how wonderful it is to be on the beach and walk on beautiful, warm, sunny days. It also adds a dimension to life when we have days of clouds, so then, when the sun comes out again, it seems even greater and more exciting to have the sun again. There is something about us wanting something that is not so readily available. I keep getting the sense more and more that there is such a wonderful opportunity we have here living on the planet that we may not get in other places. It's all about being aware of it, and being grateful for it while here, one moment at a time, one day at a time.

It reminds me of all the many places I have lived and visited. Each one seems to have things that are wonderful about it and things that are not so great. It is a matter of which we choose to look at while there. Usually we start to see what is so great after we leave. Why not fully experience it while we are there?

Like the Big Island was so beautiful and I really loved it, but I missed having the long flat beaches to walk on like near my sister's in Florida. I loved the quietness and the lack of commercialism on the Big Island. But here in New Jersey and New York, I remember how wonderful it is to have so many choices of stores to browse through so you're bound to find what you want. There are also long beaches to walk on, museums and cultural activity. It takes a lot of awareness to focus on all the beauty here we are surrounded with where ever we are and find value in each situation.

Tell me, Bear, more now of what you focus on in your work.

Well, one thing I enjoy here is that I have a more global focus. Whereas while I lived on the earth, I rarely had a whole earth focus except when perhaps you would send a blessing to the earth in our meditations. Now here my work is focused on the whole earth. It's exciting for me in the sense that it is like a big project that can benefit many people. And many of these beings are associated with me in some way, as part of my large spiritual group, like a family, that I had no idea I belonged to when I was on the planet. In fact, if people were more aware that they were part of huge groups of beings, there would be no loneliness on the planet. But that is part of the divine plan - that people forget where they come from so they can have those experiences on the planet. I guess some people get so stuck in the energy, like I did in my own life. I had stopped moving in the direction that would have most benefited me in my life. You had very gently brought to my attention how I had quite often chose to feel sorry for myself. I would try to elicit sympathy from others as a way of feeling love. I had to realize in the long run it was not advantageous to me. At least at the end I was doing it more consciously and I could laugh at my tendencies. I believe that had been part of the problem with my heart.

I carried around that feeling in my heart for so long of feeling sorry, that it weakened my heart rather than strengthened it.

Do you not have a total realization now of the patterns of your life here on earth or is it just my interpretations of the words you're using? I would think, honey, that you would know for sure what the issues around your heart were while you were here on earth.

(Multidimensional Beings)

Well, Bee, there is a complication in the sense that there is just not one factor involved. There are many that need to be taken into consideration, as I mentioned before; we are multidimensional beings. There is so much more that is happening than we realize. Just like in a car, there is not just one thing that makes it run.

There wasn't just one thing with my heart. There were the issues of genetics which goes along with certain patterns of behavior anyway. I chose that family to come into in order to work through tendencies that I already had. It helped me in my life when I learned that we came into the earth plane choosing our parents and the significant things that would happen to us to experience and learn from. I had been somewhat upset that my parents divorced when I was young, and having to live with the type of stepfather I had, but as you and I reviewed my life, I could see how there were things that my stepfather taught me that my blood father never would have been able to. I also realized how hard my mother tried to keep her life together through those times and how selfish I had been at the time, wanting all her attention. Going back and reviewing one's life at those points where we ever felt like a victim and instead see what value we gained is quite healing. Especially once one realizes we chose to go through those experiences. It would be like choosing to take a class and then instead of learning what there is new to learn just complaining about the class. Yes that is why we took the class, (or came to the planet) to learn what we still need to learn.

Each of us has different lessons, that is why we can't judge another wisely unless we have the perception to see exactly what their lesson is. It would have been like you starting your art class and judging yourself right from the beginning, complaining you didn't know how to paint like Rembrandt. Well, that is why you're in a class, to gain from the experience of learning step by step what it takes to get to that point. You may not get to paint exactly like him, but you could reach a point where you can paint from the same level with your own level of personal expression. An important point here is that each person has their own level of personal expression. So each person is unique.

Another difficulty on the planet is that people try to feel comfortable by being the same as others, which was also my tendency; to want to be like everyone else so I could fit in. That is when I started to get involved with drinking and smoking. For me, I was looking for others to give me a sense of belonging because I didn't feel that within myself. I quite often didn't live my truth so I could fit in.

I know there are also people on the planet that are so set on being different that their lessons are that they need to let go more, to fit in more, so as not to set themselves so apart from people. These are ways among the many that have different lessons. If we see someone that really sticks out from a group, unless we have the vision of their soul, we cannot judge to say, "oh, they should try to fit in more" or "they are just trying to get attention," where in reality it may be right along with their divine plan to do things differently than the majority of the group.

What can also happen with that same person is that instead of honoring the way they are, they feel sorry for themselves because they are different. They dis-empower themselves by feeling less-than everyone else. Hopefully, at some time they will be able look back and be grateful they were different and did their own thing.

There are so many different patterns; it is best to accept each situation, as far as how we are in it. Then we can tell how we feel inside and decide what parts we want to stay the way they are and what we want to change. All humans have an inner guidance system that they can tune into any time. It guides us in the areas that would benefit us to change. It is just a matter of forming a relationship to it and trusting it. How powerful humans would be if they were trained from a young age to follow that inner voice.

You were very good honey at following your inner voice and were a great motivation for me to get in touch

Bear, I think this part about all of us experiencing life on different dimensions is very helpful to understand. I guess it also could be said as living life on different levels simultaneously. It is like there is a part of me that could see that your death had to have a higher spiritual meaning beyond what I knew at the time. That didn't stop my emotions from fully experiencing the sadness. My body had no desire for food whatsoever; I didn't eat for a week. I lived on spirulina drinks just so I knew at least I was taking some nutrition into my body. My mind was totally jumbled quite often for a while. And my personality would pop in and out of its normal happy self. I could sense a part of me was having a profound experience, and it wasn't good or bad, just an amazing experience. Another part of me kept looking for what I was going to have to learn. There were so many levels going on inside me that all didn't agree with each other. It seems part of the healing process has been bringing all these parts of myself into alignment and acceptance.

So, honey what else are you doing there with your work?

(We all contribute to the whole)

As I said before, the great thing is having a feeling of helping people on a worldwide scale. I always did enjoy the feeling of helping others, so in that sense I feel really good about what I am doing. And I always loved working with friends and it is great because there is such a large group of us working together. I also see more, the importance of my own individuality, as far as making a contribution with the knowledge of my own unique vibration.

Each spirit, each being, each soul, has something to contribute to the whole. Like in the car, again, one part is not necessarily greater than the other part; each part contributes to making the car run. The body is great and is very important, yet without the battery it would not run. So one is just as great as the other, and you can go on and on with all the cars different compo-

With my individual experience and recent experience on the planet, and knowing some of the needs of the planet from my own viewpoint as a human, I have a lot to contribute to what we are all working on toward earthly transformations. How much higher quality my life on earth would have been if I had those same realizations then. It's easier for me to see it in myself here.

We are all about raising the vibrations on the planet to bring it more in alignment with the divine plan of a heaven on earth. We search for ways to assist in ways that do not interfere with human's free will to make decisions about their life, but we can do things that can influence them. And then there are of course those on the planet, many in fact, that consciously ask in many ways for assistance from us in these dimensions. People ask in many different ways according to their belief structure.

It is really a wonderful experience to be able to see so much of the world at one time in my awareness and be aware of so many different levels at one time. There are times like now where I am just mainly focused on one spot on the earth, as I am in communication with you, although I still have other awareness' happening simultaneously. What is really incredible is when I can focus on the earth and have this awareness of the whole earth and all its people and inhabitants at once. It is such an expanding feeling.

On earth things seem more finite and smaller; here I have the greater awareness and I can choose a much wider field of awareness. There is so much wonder and so much to expand into and explore. Although I am happy for you and our place together, I have visions of you being here and us exploring the realms of existence here. It is similar to how we felt when we would explore Hawaii together, both the land and the sea. There really is so much to explore and expand into on the earth.

The earth is such a beautiful planet, and we are working in the direction to keep its beauty and to heal it back into its natural state of purity. The more people realize and appreciate the beauty of the planet, the more they will have the awareness to keep it that way. That is why we are working on raising the vibrations so that everyone can fall into the flow that keeps things in that order. It is not that what has happened to the planet should be labeled as bad; it's just used as feedback on a grander scale as the appropriate steps to take toward a nicer place to live.

Beauty is an energy that is uplifting and although different people have a different viewpoint on what beauty is, the beauty of nature can be inspiring. A murky- colored river with dead fish on the shore and litter trashed all over is not a representation of beauty. I used to think at one time you were being really picky about not appreciating the fact that I would throw the cigarette butts out in the street, yet I did realize at a deep level that it was not something that was best for me to do. If all the people that smoked on the planet did that one thing, of just being aware of not uncon- sciously throwing cigarette butts all over, it would make a big difference to the planet.

So tell me more about the colors.
(Setting the Intention)
What I have been saying by communicating all this

to you, Bee, is that it is more than just working with the colors. It is working in a group energy with the intention of doing something to uplift the planet. As you remember, when we did healing work it was the intention that was set that was so much a part of the work. So, setting our intention to work together as a group for the benefit of the earth is so much of it. We transmit our energy into our work and then find ways that can reach the physical dimension. Colors and Sounds are great transmitters because we have them here and you have them there. They can be seen in similar patterns, although here things are more vibrant, and in the denseness of the earth vibration some of the vibrancy is lost. It is like figuring out a complicated math problem if this is like this here what will that be like there. And of course there is always the free-will ability that can throw off the results of our predictions.

We do work in war zones where there are people fighting, to try to get some color vibrations in there. Quite often those areas are very gray, dull or barren. There are such chaotic energies around wars because people are in such confusion. They have their inner voices that *are guiding them in one direction and yet they have such other conflicting viewpoints that confuse them, and so much of them cut off their flow. There are so many areas on the planet that can use the extra assistance of bringing in other vibrations to balance out what is going on.*

There are political areas, people's homes, cities, homeless areas, areas of starving people, high crime areas, less evolved human areas, and I could go on and on. There is a tremendous amount of work going on to bring in different vibrations to balance out what is happening now, so people can be more in a space to live a balanced life, to be more in touch with their own inner guidance by having some quiet spaces.

(Following Inner Guidance)

Bear, I saw a perfect example of that today. My sister and I have been meditating every morning going higher into the light, similarly to what you and I did. I know you know this because I always connect with you when we do this. But in the meditation we have been praying that she learn to be more at peace with school instead of being so stressed about getting good grades. A big step for her was to take off Monday, miss her class, and be okay with it. During the meditation, she saw herself telling the teacher what we did and saw him responding to her by telling her it was okay; every once in a while one needs just to take off and do something like that. Normally she would assume the teacher would be upset because she missed the class. Today, when she finally saw her teacher, she told him why she missed class and he had the same response she saw in the meditation. Her inner guidance was telling her it was okay to do what she was doing, then the physical world confirmed it.

I have been working on following my inner guidance for years, and have been putting much conscious attention to doing so. It was my main motivation in taking the spiritual development class at Delphi. Contacting inner guidance was one of the claims of the class. I had been feeling for some time, that the best tool for me to have for a successful life is to be able to trust my inner voice. Although I experienced this many times before that, since I was nineteen, and had taken the Silva Mind Development training, I just had to keep working on developing it to a point where I was "confident" in it.

Now I can go back to times when I was seven, remembering very clearly once when my dad made a wrong turn while driving. I knew he was going the wrong way, but I didn't feel confident enough in myself to say anything, so I kept quiet as he ended up getting lost. I have now grown a tremendous confidence in my intuition, yet still I get tested. At these times it is about letting go and trusting, always remembering <u>I am taken care of, always have been, and will be by the Universe.</u>

In fact, last night in my meditation, more of that came up. I just surrendered to the universe and trusted. It is all about trusting. There seems nothing greater I can trust than my inner voice. I saw in my last Trance Dance insight that you were a part of me trusting the universe. I know I can trust you; I can allow the experience of trust into my life and through you I can transpose that onto all other parts of my life. It is as if you're the representative of God for me in the line of trust.

(the play on death)

Thank you, Bee, for trusting me. Yes, from here we

can see that all can be trusted, for what is there to fear? Since there is no death, why would one fear it? It would be like an actor on a stage saying, "I don't want to play the part of someone dying because I am afraid." That would be very unusual because the actor knows he is not really going to die. After the show is over, he is going to get up and go on with his life. It is the same with death. What is there to fear after you go through the play of death on the earth? People are going to get up and continue on with their lives in another way than they did before. Things will just be somewhat shifted. It could also be compared to leaving one country, sleeping on the plane, waking up and then leaving the plane to live in a totally different country with a different lifestyle. The fear of death interferes with many people living their life fully trying to avoid the inevitable. Even with you, my Bee, though you didn't fear your own death, you did fear mine. How much different life would be if death were just accepted as easily as someone deciding they wanted to take a nap or go visit another country. I know, Bee, for us it was just we really wanted to be together, and you just wanted us to be able to stay together and enjoy each others company, and we are, just in a different way than we expected to.

I know, Bear, still when I hear the song from Aladdin that we used on our wedding day about how my life with you is a whole new world, I never imagined it could expand into so great an area of new worlds. I love watching our wedding video and watching us sing that song to each other.

"You Bee, you..." that really was such a beautiful day of our lives; all the energy and attention we put into that day to create a special day for the celebration of our love really paid off in many ways. You were so beautiful and radiant and I was so proud to call you my wife - my "wifee" Bee. It was a fun and exciting day. Celebrating days of joy on the planet is very beneficial. We have celebrations here also as people celebrate on the planet. We are really interconnected in many ways that people do not realize.

Bear, is there anything else you want to communicate? (your consciousness is your life)

Bee, I cannot tell you enough of the radiance of your beauty. To me you're like an angel on the planet, like a shining star in the night, like the Bee that spreads its pollen from flower-to-flower and then makes sweet, sweet honey like nectar of the gods. If you could see your magnificence as I do, you would never doubt who you are or what your place is in the world. Imagine how you feel when you are at your best - like when you're teaching or doing healing work, and you feel totally connected to your spirit as you are in the flow. This is how I see you all the time. This is who I know you are. Yes, you're still finding your way and making what would be called mistakes. But there is no need for judgment upon yourself. Your search to rise above judgment starts with yourself and seeing who you also are on a higher level, and seeing and being in the sense of who you are in the higher light. As you connect more in the light through meditation or through gratitude, you naturally bring your own energy into a vibration where you see from this level. Your prayers are very helpful to you as you continue to pray to see the world through these eyes. It would be helpful for you to realize it would also benefit you to connect with your own higher self and look at the world through these eyes, anchoring this energy more into your daily life. Ask in your prayers that you may live more regularly from this point of view.

Thank you, Bear, for your guidance. How grateful I am for you in my life just as I was when you were here in the physical. Even more so though, now I am open to hearing your words of wisdom. How different the world looks when we are in that space. It amazed me when we would meditate and you would have one viewpoint when we went into meditation and another when we came out; you had connected with the higher energies. I am amazed myself when I look at something from one point of view and then change my consciousness. My point of view totally changes about the same situation. Life really does seem to be a reflection of where our consciousness is in our life.

Anything else, Bear, you would like to communicate? (Life beyond earth)

Yes, dear one; our work together at this time is to show by example some of the struggles of living on the earth plane and getting through those struggles with the assistance of inner guidance at some level. You're really the one getting through the earth struggles, and

I am a support system for you to remind you it is not as dreadful an experience as it might seem. I can help to remind you of the value of the experiences, although you do and usually have been very good at seeing the good in any situation. It is also very important for people living on the planet to realize there is a much greater expanded point of view than one's personal life on earth. When one dies and looks back at their life, they do not judge their success by how much money they made but by how much love was in their heart. There is a whole planet that all are connected to and there is life after earth or beyond earth. Also, that love never dies but lives on and on.

We will continue to work together in different ways throughout the rest of your life on earth, which includes more writing at another time period as you continue on with your other life experiences. I am one of your guides and am grateful for this opportunity to be able to watch over you. You're safe in the world, dear one, and I am with you.

Thank you, Bear. How wonderful it has been these last

days writing this information from you and it has been happening so naturally. I am grateful to God for you in my life
and in these writings. I pray that our experiences together
and these writings may touch people deeply to inspire them
in some way to live life more fully, and that we may be chan-
nels of healing on this planet. As you know, Bear, when we
got married and did those healings together it was fulfilling my dream of having a partner in my life that would
work by my side. And here you are working by me, side-
by-side. I guess next time I should be more specific and
specify it to be in the physical. Just a little humor, honey. I
love you just the way you are and am forever grateful to
you, and for the universe for allowing us to live together on
the earth, in the physical, even if it was just a short time.

Until next time....

Closure

December 18

Dear Bear,

I know it has been a while since I wrote. I feel now it is best to close these writings for now. I have my life to live and you have yours. I know we will still be in communication at some level. You're forever in my heart. Thank you again, dear one, for all the love we have shared. Your spirit will continue to make me smile and glow; a glorious, gracious, loving glow.... that only a Bee and a Bear can share. May your life in the spirit world be filled with the love of the angels, many colors beyond our rainbow, and the celestial music that soothes all souls.

Until we meet again,

In love and light,

Loryn

Letter Writing for Healing

Dear Friends,

I have found that letter writing to a loved one who is no longer in our life can be a very healing experience, whether they have passed away or moved away. I suggest you write one to allow a feeling of completion to take place in your relationship. The following are suggestions for phrases you can use in your letters. Before you begin, remember a time when you felt close to this person and then sense they are in the room with you as you write. Feel the love in your heart.

Dear ....,

Some of the things I would like to tell you are:

I wish that....

I am sorry that....

I wish I had told you that....

 I am angry that.....(it is natural and okay to have some anger)

It has been very challenging for me to........

Please forgive me for....

I forgive you for......

I am sad that.....

I feel ....

I know......

I loved that ....

If I had another day with you I would......

What I have learned is ....

The good thing is......

From now on I will.....

Thank you for........

I am grateful that........

If I could sense what you would want to communicate to
me it would be ....

Love,

....

286

Meditation for Healing the Broken Heart

Dear Friends,

When a loved one dies (or leaves), for many of us it feels as if a part of our heart goes with them. It can feel like a part of us dies. We can change that. We need to have all our spiritual energy to live our life on earth to the best of our ability, to live full, vibrant lives being grateful for our life on earth. We need to call our energy back and heal the wound. We are not being valiant or more loving by allowing a part of ourselves to die with them. That happens from a lack of knowledge of the truth of life.

The truth of life is that love never dies and no distance can change that. If you're living with a dear one and they move away, the love does not die; only the form of the relationship changes. We must always respect our loved one's path and realize their path may at some time in our life go in a different direction than ours, whether it be beloved, parent, friend, sibling, or child. This is where a greater love comes in, a love that comes with respect and honor, rather than fearing if they leave we will not be able to survive.

The healing comes when we can change our perspective and realize our love for them is within our hearts. We can go within and feel that love at any time we choose and feel them within us. Every relationship changes. Even if you have a child, the infant no longer exists; do we cry because the child we held in our arms is not there? No, we realize they have grown up and a new form takes place and the relationship changes as the form changes.

So it is when someone dies. Their physical form changes and their spirit lives on. Their spirit may have a place to be near us and watch over us as we continue to live on the earth, either for a short time, at certain challenging or special times or for the rest of our lives, just like we have friends and relatives on earth that are around a lot or come around on and off in cycles.

Feeling sadness for the loss of a loved one right now is a

natural part of our life cycle as a human being. It is necessary that we experience all ranges of human emotions to live a full human life. There is a time for sadness, but then it must cycle back up into a time of joy and each person moves at their own rate. I think we have to be careful not to get stuck; we must move totally into the sadness and then back into the joy.

I believe in our society we are prone to avoid sadness. We believe that it is a sign of weakness to be sad or cry. This is not so! It is a sign you're living in a human body with human emotions, but in order to get through it you must go into it. So go into it, and then get out of it. If you try to avoid it by not talking about it or thinking about it, it will just linger around for years, and you and those close to you will lose precious time on earth to be joyful.

In this meditation, when you go into your heart, if you feel sadness first, it is okay. If you haven't allowed yourself to feel much then stay with it a while, but then make sure you move into the healing part and spend a long time strengthening and reconnecting the bond of love.

May your love be realized.

The meditation: You can guide yourself through it or read

this into a tape and play it.

Close your eyes. Either sit or lie down. You may want to put on some soft, relaxing, music. Take three very slow deep breaths, inhaling and exhaling to the count of seven. Imagine yourself surrounded by a column of light. This light comes from the great central sun, the heavens, the source of all light and moves through you deep down into the heart of the earth. Imagine an elevator of spiritual light run by a beautiful spiritual being, an angel perhaps. Tell this being you would like to move to the level where you can reconnect with your loved one. This being acknowledges your request and sends a telepathic message to your loved one. This being is the guardian of the gate and will give you the okay to proceed.

Once the okay has been given, sense yourself moving up in this elevator, going higher and higher; feeling yourself getting lighter and lighter as you move upward, feeling an anticipation of your reunion. You feel yourself lighter and lighter, feeling freer and freer like a bird soaring through the skies under the sun. As the elevator continues to go higher and higher you think of your loved one and remember a time you felt close to them, calling out their name (out loud) three times, the name you used to call them, feeling love in your heart as you do so. See angels outside the column assisting with their energy as you continue to lift higher and higher into more light, feeling more and more love in your heart continuing to feel lighter and lighter, sensing this elevator of light going higher and higher moving to the level where you can once again meet with your loved one. The elevator stops, the door opens, your loved one is in front of you, greeting you with love in their heart and a smile on their face Give them a hug.

See, sense, or feel their presence with you. Remember and feel the love that exists in your heart for them. Give them the gift of your love. Imagine your love as a ray of light or energy flowing from your heart to theirs. This gives them joy to feel your connection with them. Realize the sadness you have felt is the acceptance of the thought that they haven't been near you. Realize now that as you feel the connection of this love that this is the truth, that this love exists always within your heart so that you may tap into it whenever you choose. Feel the love, feel the connection. Feel the sadness and you will close yourself off to this love within your heart. If you cannot feel a love connection ask that forgiveness take place and feel the peace. Feel the love, feel the depth of connection that you have with this being that goes beyond this world you live in. Ask within your heart that this bond of love be healed and made stronger, so that whenever you remember this being you will feel them so strongly within your own heart that you no longer miss their presence, because you're now able to carry this love around within you always. Now your bond may even feel stronger than when they lived on earth. Sense their joy to know you're happy and re-connected with them. Realize it was not them that left you but perhaps you that thought the love no longer was there. Feel the love, feel the connection. Feel the love, feel the connection. Sense if there is something they may want to communicate to you. Be open to receive a message. It may feel like it is only your imagination, because your imagination is the vehicle they use for the communication. Be open to also receiving communication from them in your dreams.

As you feel this love so deeply in your heart, remember your pain from the past and realize that many human beings are still in pain, although they may appear to be strong. Remember all human beings need love and compassion, no matter how strong they appear on the outside. Remind yourself to be a more compassionate human being. Now with this everlasting love strengthened within your own heart, see yourself as a beacon of love moving out into the world having a greater sense of the depth of the human soul. Realize the gift you have to continue to live on the earth in a physical body. See yourself living your life with a more grateful heart for the loved ones around you that you're still able to share a physical world with. Feel the appreciation of your human existence.

Recognize that their death has given you an opportunity, in some way to become much wiser or stronger. Accept this gift and do the best you can with it. Honor them by being the best you can be and by honoring the love you have with them that cannot be threatened. Feel the love, honor the love, be grateful for the love, know that this love is and always shall be through all time and all space, now and forever.

Stay in this energy of love with them as long as you wish. When you're ready, thank them for sharing this love with you. Go back into the celestial elevator, allow it to gently bring you back down to the earth plane. Thank the celestial beings. Bring your awareness back into the room with your

heart comforted and filled with gratitude.

My Invitation

Nov. 28, 1997

Dear Friend,

It has been exactly two years, three months, and three weeks since Rock's spirit left his body. I have had many changes in my life, all for the better. I have become wiser, stronger, more loving, more grateful, more compassionate, more intuitive, and more understanding. I still communicate with the other side through letters to a group of spiritual friends I call the Council of Nine. I feel Rock around me often and we occasionally write letters.

I am living again in Florida, enjoying the sunshine, warm weather, beaches, and the dolphins that frequent our backyard lagoon.

I will soon be starting to train to be a hospice volunteer. I have been connecting people with the voice of their souls and doing spiritual counseling. I began to set classes up to teach yoga, meditation, and spiritual development. I have been holding sacred Trance Dance events for people to dance with their soul, energy healing workshops, and discussions and healings on afterlife issues. The life-after-death classes are dear to my heart. I see many people dealing with the pain of the loss of a loved one and am grateful to be able to share with others what has helped me with my own healing process, hoping it will help them.

An amazing thing is that half of the people in my classes feel they have received some communication from their deceased loved ones. I have heard some amazing stories about these communications. Many have been much more phenomenal than mine, like electrical things going on and off when they were not plugged in. I have noticed it helps people to be able to talk about their own story. This can be difficult if those around you feel uncomfortable discussing the topic, so I invite you to share your stories and letters with me. Hearing your stories helps me to give others confirmation on those that have had experiences similar to yours.

May love, truth, balance, harmony, beauty, and peace
fill all your lives.

Blessings to you all,

Loryn Solana Walton

Write to: Solstar
P.O. Box 320987
Cocoa Beach, FL 32932-0987
Attention: Solana
Solstarpub@aol.com

Closing Letter

February 20, 2000

Dear Reader,

I have carried you, the reader, around in my heart these past two years as the publishing of Letters Through The Veil was temporarily postponed. In the meantime I made copies of it at the request of my students and clients. I am grateful that this now expanded version of the book is being professionally published. The gratitude expressed from those first readers inspired my perseverance to widely distribute the book.

Things have been going well in my life as I regularly meditate, pray, practice yoga, and refine my vegetarian diet to create a deeper inner peace. Continuing to work through life's challenges I am growing spiritually. While meditating, a vision of the Blessed Mother came to me. Here I felt a deep love and acceptance and recognized her as a symbol of honoring the feminine energy of the planet. She later guided me to pray the Rosary as I did as a child. However, this time the power of its mysteries was revealed to me. The Blessed Mother then guided me back to church to connect with the Christ Consciousness through Holy Communion. There the realization came that church could be a more powerful experience by praying to feel Christ within me and interpreting the deeper meaning of the scriptures and the mass. I have also returned to the teachings of Paramahansa Yogananda. He was a great holy man from India, who taught the unity of the Eastern philosophies and Western religions. He taught God could be personally experienced through meditation and prayer. Through practicing this form of meditation I sit each day and am filled with the bliss of feeling God in my heart. His insights into the teachings of Jesus Christ help me better understand my Christian religious upbringing. His philosophy of yoga further inspired my continued interest in that topic.

To further facilitate my spiritual growth I have been recording the insights I've received through my dreams and meditations. These insights are a guide in my journey through the lessons of life. An important lesson I have learned is to create ways on a daily basis to live more spiritually. One way I achieve this is by using my spiritual name "Solana". It was a name received while meditating, meaning "One with the Divine Light." I use it as a reminder to live in the essence of my true being - a child of God. I am still finding ways to generate more joy in my life. I continue to love my long walks on the beach. I have made peace with Agatha and on occasion am reminded of Rock as a spiritual guide. My new spiritual partner also adds more joy and blessings in my life.

I am at the beginning of a new phase of my spiritual development. I have enrolled in another level of yoga teachers training in California. Advanced classes in developing my intuitive and healing abilities will take place in Georgia. Finally, I will be going to a new medical intuitive training program in St. Louis. I would love to tell you more but space and time does not permit. Perhaps another time, another place, another book . . .

Love and Blessings to all,

Solana

About the Author

Loryn "Solana" Walton has been an international teacher and speaker in the body, mind, and spirit field for over 20 years, including being a former instructor of the international Silva Mind Development Training.

She is an Ordained Minister in the Church of Wisdom, a certified medium, and holds several yoga teacher certifications. Her studies have led her through many forms of healing methods, including being a Reiki Master and Ro-Hun Therapist.

Resources
Classes and Workshops

Delphi Retreat Center
PO Box 70
McCaysville, GA 30555
706-492-2772
888-335-7448
registrar@delphi-center.com
www.delphi-center.com

Monroe Institute
PO Box 505
Lovingston, VA 22949
800-541-2488
www.monroe-inst.com

Frank Natale
Morgan Road
409 N. Pacific Coast Hwy. #465
Redondo Beach, CA 90277
310-281-1705
Natale@morganroad.com
www.morganroad.com

Omega Institute
260 Lake Dr.
Rhinebeck, NY 12572
800-944-1001
914-266-4444
www.omega-inst.org

Art of Conscious Loving
PO box 69
Paia, Maui, Hawaii 96779
808-572-8364
tantra@mauigateway.com
www.sourcetantra.com

Satchidananda Ashram
Yogaville
Buckingham, Virginia 23921
800-858-YOGA (9642)
804-969-3121
800-476-1347 (for catalog of products)
www.yogaville.org

Body*Mind*Spirit Center for Healthy Living
932 D Preston Ave
Charlotsville, VA 22903
804- 984-9700
life@spiritandbody.com
www.spiritandbody.com

Silva Mind Development
PO Box 2249
1407 Calle Del Norte
Laredo, TX 78944-2249
956-722-6390
800-545-6463
www.silvamethod.com

Micky Trione (artist)
BlueChroma@aol.com

Sunseeker (charter adventure)
Big Island of Hawaii
PO Box 383657
Waikoloa, HI 96738
808-883-8847 Captain Paul Warren
808-325-8221

Georgia Shakti-Hill
PO Box 2715
Ft.Myers, FL 33932-2715
941-463-8088
www.shakti-hill.com

Wisdom Channel
www.wisdom.com

National Hospice Organization
1901 North More Street Suite 901
Arlington, VA 22209
800-658-8898
www.nho.org

Self-Realization Fellowship
3880 San Rafael Ave.
Los Angeles, CA 90065-3298
323-225-2471
www.yogananda-srf.org

Linda Shurman - Astrologer
4016 Hermitage Drive
Voorhees, NJ 08043
856-874-1651
www.soothesayer.com

Debra S. Ritchey
Astrology/Intuitive
6080 S. Hulen #360-303
Fort Worth, TX 76132
817-443-0350
DSR4star@aol.com

Recommended Reading

The following is a list of some of my favorite authors and titles that reflect many of the topics in this book.

Albright, Judith. *Our Lady of Medjugorje.* The Riehle Foundation.

Alexander, Thea. *2150 A.D.* New York: Warner Books, 1976

*Bach, Richard. *Bridge across Forever.* William Morrow and Co. 1984

Brendan, Jason. *Peace at Last,* After-Death Experience of John Lennon. Illumination Arts 1989

*Chopra, Deepak. *Higher Self.* (audio)

*Dyer, Wayne. *Real Magic, Creating Miracles in Everyday Life.* Harper, 1993

Eadie, J. Betty. *Embraced By The Light.* Bantam Books, 1994

Gibran, Kahil. *The Prophet.*

*Gawain, Shakti. *Creative Visualization.* New York Bantam, 1982

Harvey, Andrew. *Son of Man: The Direct Way to Christ.* JPT

Jorde, Krista & Rocha, Adriana. *A Child of Eternity: An Extraordinary Young Girl's Message from the World Beyond.* Ballentine Books, 1995.

*King, Godfre Ray. *Magic Presence.* Saint Germain Press, 1935.

MacLaine, Shirley. *Out on a Limb.* New York Bantam, 1983.

*Moen, Larry. *Meditations for Healing.* US Publishing

*Monroe, Robert. *Ultimate Journey.* Main Street Books, 1996.

Montfort, St. Louis de. *Secret of the Rosary.* Monfort Publications, 1965.

Muir, Charles and Caroline. *Art of Conscious Loving.* Mercury House, 1990.

*Myss, Caroline. *Anatomy of the Spirit.*

Natale, Frank. *Trance Dance:The Dance of Life.* Book and CD edition, Element, 1995.

Parrish-Harra, Rev. Carol E. *The Aquarian Rosary.* Sparrow Hawk Press, 1988.

*Radha, Swami Sivanada. *Realities of the Dreaming Mind.*

*Riso, Don Richard. *Personality Types.* Houghton Mufin Co 1987,1996.

*Roberts, Jane. *Oversoul Seven Trilogy.* Amber Allen Publishing.

*Roman, Sanaya. *Soul Love: Awakening your Heart Centers.* HJ Kramer, 1997.

Roth, Ron. *Healing Path to Prayer.*

*Satchidanda, Sri Swami. Golden Present Integral Yoga Press.

Shakti-Hill, Georgia. *Sharing the Light.* Shakti-Hill Publishing, 1998.

Shumway, D. Injeeai. *Reflections on a Dream.*

Smith Marshall and Patricia Hayes. *Extension of Life.*

Spalding, Baird. *Life and Teaching of the Masters of the Far East,* Volume 1-5. DeVorss and Co. 1924, 1937, 1964.

*Stearn, Jess. *Power of Alpha Thinking.* William Morrow and Company 1976, 1989.

Szekely, B. Edmond. *Essene Gospel of Peace, Book One.* IBS Intl 1981.

Tomioka, A. *On the Breath of the Gods: A Journey into the Heart of Love.* HELI.

Van Praagh, James. *Talking to Heaven: A Medium's Message of Life after Death.*

Whitfield, Joseph. *Eternal Quest: A Mystical Story of Love.* TREA

*Yogananda, Paramahansa. *Autobiography of a Yogi,* Self-Realization 1979.

Yogi Ramacharaka. *Science of Breath.* Yogi Publication Society 1940.

Zolar. *Ro-Hun; Dancing Heart to Heart.*

*also recommended other books by same author.

Recommended Music and Musicians

<u>Light and Joyful:</u> Dancing with my Soul by Ayman Sawaf
Light Transitions by Steve Smith through Delphi

<u>To move to:</u> Shamans Breath by Professor Trance and the Energizers (trance dance)
Zone Unknown by Gabrielle Roth
Enigma by Enigma

<u>Heart:</u> Enya by Enya
Love all the Way by Matisha

<u>Tantra:</u> Music to Disappear In (Two) Hearts of Space by Raphael
Kama Sutra by Shah
Enhancing Intimacy by Steve Halpern

<u>Spiritually Uplifting:</u> Music to Disappear In by Raphael
Atlantis Angelis, Solaris Universalis by Patrick Bernhardt

<u>Meditative:</u> Om by Brother Charles

<u>Relaxing Music:</u> Spectrum Suite by Steve Halpern (all music by Halpern)
Raku by PC Davidoff
Pachelbel Canyon by various artists

<u>Chanting, Christian & Gregorian:</u> Alleluia, Gloria by Robert Gass
Chant by Benedictine Monks

<u>Chanting, Eastern:</u> Radha Krishna Temple by Bhakivedanta Society
Ananda by Howard Beckman
Pilgram Heart by Krisha Das
Integral Yoga Kirtan by Swami Satchidananda

<u>World Music:</u> Deep Forest by Deep Forest

<u>Spiritually Uplifting:</u> Ghandarva Experience by Tom Kenyon

Recommended Movies:

Ghost
Made In Heaven
Gillians 37th Birthday
Heart and Souls
Always
Defending Your Life
What Dreams May Come
The Sixth Sense

Recommended Television:

Touched by an Angel
Oprah Winfrey Show

<u>Glossary</u>

<u>11:11</u>: January 11- represents an opening of a new doorway into higher dimensions for the earth.

<u>Chakra system</u>: energy centers within the body. The seven major ones are the root, source of physical energy; the spleen-emotional energy; the solar plexus; power center; heart; love center; throat; communication center; third eye, spiritual sight; crown; source of spiritual energy.

<u>Channel of Healing</u>: opening to the flow of Divine energy to channel through into someone or something else.

<u>Cloud Beings</u>: a group of Spiritual beings that live on another dimension than ours and appear as clouds.

<u>Dark Night of the Soul</u>: a spiritual passage of time when we feel totally alone in the world.

<u>Delphi</u>: University and healing retreat center.

<u>Energy Healing</u>: laying on of hands using Divine Energy flow.

<u>Enneagram</u>: an ancient spiritual system using nine personality types to understand ourselves. They are the perfectionist, the helper, the achiever, the artist, the knower, the loyalist, the jack of all trades, the leader and the peacemaker.

<u>Firewalk</u>: walking over hot coals to overcome fears and realize the power of the mind.

<u>Five rhythms</u>: represent different rhythms of life, such as the passive, the chaotic, the melodic, the sharp, the light, etc.

<u>Focus 21</u>: a high level of consciousness where quite often

one can meet their deceased loved ones.

<u>Healing Evening</u>: an evening where groups of healers come and offer hands on healing to those in need of some spiritual energy.

<u>Higher Selves</u>: a higher aspect of ourselves, all loving and wise.

<u>Journeying</u>: traveling to other states of consciousness in meditation.

<u>Pleiadians</u>: group of spiritual beings from star system in Taurus constellation here to assist humans.

<u>Power animal</u>: Shamanic symbol for strength and power.

<u>Psychic attacks</u>: negative energy can attack on a non-physical level.

<u>Psychic Surgeon</u>: has the ability to go into the body without cutting tools and pull out toxic matter.

<u>Ro-Hun</u>: removal of negative thought patterns, etheric thought surgery.

<u>Sacred Rituals</u>: ceremonies.

<u>Shaman</u>: can be compared to an American Indian medicine man.

<u>Shamanism</u>: Believes the imagination provides a window into powerful realities and uses those realities to make changes in this one.

<u>Shamanic journey</u>: an active meditation used to go into other realms to gain information helpful to this one, usually to gain some kind of personal strength or power.

<u>Silva Mind Development</u>: Thorough course on training and learning the power of the mind.

<u>Soul Hunting</u>: a shamanistic belief that traumatic events

make part of our soul or spirit leave the body and not want
to come back until we coax it back and let it know things
will be okay.

Soul quality: our unique qualities our soul is developing or
experiencing.

Sweat Lodge: a sacred American Indian tradition in enclosed
areas, like tepees, using hot coals and steam (like steam
room) to sweat out the unwanted and pray for all those involved including the earth and all its creatures. The challenge to stay in the hot area assists us in feeling the depth
of our desire for a new outcome.

Tantra: an ancient Eastern tradition of combining male and
female energy in a sacred way to grow closer through love
to the Divine.

Tarot: an ancient system of knowledge.

Trance: altered states of consciousness, occurring in various levels.

Trance Dance: dancing in an altered state of consciousness
to experience bliss.

Traveling to other realms in meditation: experiencing many
different dimensions.

Vedic: Hindu.

Witness: a spiritual perspective of watching self and non
attachment.

White Brotherhood: group of high level beings working on
assisting the earth, associated with the Ascended masters.

World of duality: our perception of good and bad, compared
to a unity consciousness where all is one and there is no
evil because all is God.

Index